Marco Klapper

The nature of informed option trading

Evidence from the takeover market

Anchor Academic
Publishing

Klapper, Marco: The nature of informed option trading: Evidence from the takeover market. Hamburg, Anchor Academic Publishing 2013

Buch-ISBN: 978-3-95489-172-6
PDF-eBook-ISBN: 978-3-95489-672-1
Druck/Herstellung: Anchor Academic Publishing, Hamburg, 2013

Bibliografische Information der Deutschen Nationalbibliothek:
Die Deutsche Nationalbibliothek verzeichnet diese Publikation in der Deutschen Nationalbibliografie; detaillierte bibliografische Daten sind im Internet über http://dnb.d-nb.de abrufbar.

Bibliographical Information of the German National Library:
The German National Library lists this publication in the German National Bibliography. Detailed bibliographic data can be found at: http://dnb.d-nb.de

OUTLINE

1. Introduction

Financial markets are driven by information and by individuals that generate, process, and disclose this information to the market. Naturally, there have to be individuals who possess more information about a firm or a future event than other market participants. Mergers and acquisitions are particularly interesting events in this regard because they can have significant implications for the firms and stakeholders involved, as well as for the competitive dynamics in the respective market. Because of the large potential price impact of such transactions, traders with private information about a prospective takeover are expected to trade on this information to make a profit. But who are these "informed traders" and what kind of information do they possess?

A vast body of literature deals with the value effects of mergers and acquisitions, as well as with firm characteristics that determine the size of the takeover premium. The asset pricing literature, on the other hand, is concerned with the link between stock and options markets, i.e. which of these is the primary market in the price discovery process of stocks. Research combining these two strands of the literature is, however, fairly scarce. This study elaborates on the cross-sectional relationship between options and stocks around takeover announcements. While some research has already been conducted on the predictive power of certain informed option trading proxies for takeover announcement returns, most papers are concerned with the predictability of bidder returns. Target firms are often neglected because few targets are publicly listed and even fewer have (liquid) options traded on their stock, which decreases both the sample and the statistical significance of the results. Target firms also play a smaller role in the literature because it is mainly the announcement returns of bidding firms that allow researchers to draw inferences about the wealth effects of acquisitions. However, target firms might be a lot more attractive for informed traders since target shareholders usually receive a large premium, while the returns of bidding firms are slightly negative on average.

To the best of my knowledge, no attempt has been made in the existing literature to reconcile theories on the predictability of stock returns by means of options with empirical evidence relating firm and takeover attributes to announcement returns of target firms. Why would this be relevant? If certain deal characteristics determine the size of the takeover premium, they should also affect the predictive power of options for stock returns. In other words, they may contribute to our understanding of informed trading and the role options markets play in the price discovery process of stocks. Are informed traders corporate or industry insiders? Do they have knowledge of the details about the offer terms? For example, do they know whether the takeover will be financed primarily with cash or with stocks; is the ownership structure of the target firm relevant; and how certain are informed traders that the takeover will take place? These questions constitute the conceptual framework of this study. More generally, my research question is as follows:

What information do "informed" option traders have with regard to the target firm and the deal before the official takeover announcement?

To answer this question, I merge M&A data from SDC Platinum with options and stock data from OptionMetrics and CRSP, respectively, resulting in a sample of 2,390 takeovers. Additionally, I obtain information from Compustat, I/B/E/S, and Corporate Library (all via WRDS). In a first step, I determine if option liquidity rises to abnormal levels in the five days prior to a takeover announcement. Using a logit regression model, I then try to find preliminary evidence that option liquidity proxies such as open interest and bid ask spread can predict takeovers. The results indicate that liquidity rises before an offer and that it has some predictive abilities, showing that informed trading is taking place in options markets.

Second, I replicate a recent paper by Chan et al. (2012) who use an event study, sorted quintile portfolios, and multivariate regressions to examine whether three informed option trading proxies – implied volatility spread, implied volatility skew, and the relative option-to-stock trading volume O/S – have predictive power for takeover announcement returns. For my sample of target firms, I find no evidence that the implied volatility spread is positively related to the takeover premium. Using the three-day average spread, the relationship is positive but remains insignificant. I confirm that implied volatility skew is a negative predictor of the premium. In direct contrast to the existing literature, I find the O/S ratio to be negatively – not positively – related to target announcement returns.

In the final part of this study, I interact the three informed option trading proxies with dummy variables representing certain deal characteristics. For example, I argue that cash offers should attract more informed option trading than stock offers because a cash premium is less uncertain and usually needs to be higher due to the tax advantages of stock payments. I find no firm statistical evidence that the predictive power of the three proxies is dependent on how the takeover is financed. Using proxies for managerial entrenchment, I further argue that informed traders with accurate information about the takeover would trade in options even when liquidity is low, because the expected premium is higher if target management is entrenched. On the other hand, less informed traders trade in stocks because entrenchment decreases the probability that the takeover will occur. The interaction term on the O/S ratio supports this narrative. Lastly, I show that informed trading is more pronounced if the target and the bidding firm are in the same industry, i.e. that industry know-how drives informed trading.

This study adds to the existing body of literature in several ways: (i) it combines findings from the corporate finance and asset pricing literature; (ii) it focuses on target firms where other studies investigate acquiring firms; (iii) it uses a larger sample than comparable studies; (iv) it shows that option liquidity has limited predictive power for takeover announcements; and (v) it provides some evidence that informed option trading is driven by rational agents with detailed information about future takeovers, and perhaps by industry insiders.

The remainder of this paper is organized as follows: Section 2 will summarize the relevant literature, draw a conceptual framework, and formulate a number of hypotheses; Section 3 presents the data and methodology; Section 4 discusses the empirical results; and Section 5 concludes.

2. Literature Review

This review summarizes the key contributions of the mergers and acquisition literature and adds to this literature by integrating studies on corporate finance and M&A related asset pricing. While the first part of this section focuses on theories and empirical findings related to the nature of takeover deals and the problems associated with measuring the shareholder value of these transactions, the second part delves into a more recent strand of research that relates option trading proxies to M&A announcement returns. In part 3, the findings from both fields are combined to develop a conceptual framework and to formulate a number of research hypotheses.

2.1 The value of mergers and acquisitions

2.1.1 Occurrence and characteristics

Mergers and acquisitions are among the most popular research topics in corporate finance. There is a vast literature on the value effects of these transactions as well as on the question why mergers occur in the first place. For example, Bradley et al. (1988, p. 4) suggest that the primary driving force behind mergers is "an attempt by the bidding firm to exploit a profit opportunity created by a change in economic conditions." These changes can include shifts in demand or supply, technological advances, as well as deregulation and government policy changes. In a comprehensive literature survey, Andrade et al. (2001) present other plausible explanations for the occurrence of mergers: synergy and efficiency considerations, attempts to create market power, replacement of incompetent target managers, and self-serving motives of the acquiring firm's management (personal diversification, entrenchment, hubris). The empirical literature finds evidence for the hypothesis that merger activity in the late twentieth century was to a large extent the result of economic shocks that triggered entire "waves" of takeovers. During each of these waves, the level of merger activity in some industries was higher than in others, an observation that Mitchell and Mulherin (1996) ascribe to industry-specific shocks such as deregulation and foreign competition that ultimately forced firms into restructurings. The authors hypothesize that takeovers are a relatively inexpensive way to react to a shock, as compared to internal restructurings. Andrade et al. (2001) identify U.S. industries that experienced major deregulation and, subsequently, merger activity, e.g. airlines in the late 1970s, broadcasting in the 1980s, and media/telecommunications in the 1990s. Additionally, each merger wave shows distinct characteristics such as different deal volume, degree of hostility, usage of stock as method of payment, etc.

2.1.2 EVENT STUDIES ON THE WEALTH EFFECTS OF ACQUISITIONS

2.1.2.1 ABNORMAL RETURNS METHODOLOGY

Determining the wealth effects of takeovers is a non-trivial task. Most studies fall back on Brown and Warner's (1985) basic event study methodology that assesses the impact of corporate events on share prices. The method uses daily stock return observations over a longer "estimation period" prior to the event announcement and then estimates the expected or "normal" returns for the stock during a shorter time frame around the observed event ("event period"). Normally, this is done with an ordinary least squares (OLS) regression model. The sum of the differences between actual and normal returns is commonly referred to as the cumulative abnormal return (CAR). It is a cornerstone in almost all empirical studies on corporate announcements, including mergers and acquisitions.

Brown and Warner (1985) find that the plain market model is well-specified in the context of event study methodologies, i.e. with regard to the non-normality of returns and return autocorrelation. But there are several other problems that come with this approach. For example, Andrade et al. (2001) point out that the benchmark model for estimating normal returns becomes more important for longer event periods, as expected returns can vary tremendously over long-term horizons. This issue is relevant for M&A studies since not all value effects from an announced acquisition are immediately priced in during the event period. There is always a probability that the deal will not be consummated or that another bidder will ultimately succeed in acquiring the target firm (cf. Bhagat et al. 2005). Technically, the event period should therefore include all days between the announcement and the completion date to ensure that all expected value effects are incorporated. However, this becomes unfeasible in practice as it can take several months before a merger ultimately succeeds (or fails). Extending the event window accordingly adds considerable noise to the model as other news about the merging firms enters the market. Furthermore, returns would have to be discounted over a longer event window, requiring an additional estimate of the appropriate discount rate. According to Bhagat et al. (2005), short-window event studies therefore suffer from a so-called "truncation" bias. Methods of how to isolate the pure takeover value under these circumstances will be discussed in more detail below.

As for the benchmark model, the simple market model (or CAPM) is still widely used and considered accurate enough for short event periods. However, the three- and four-factor models suggested by Fama and French (1993) and Carhart (1997), respectively, generally prove to be a better fit for the empirical data and are recommended for longer event windows as they increase the accuracy of expected return estimates.

2.1.2.2 Takeover premiums

The aforementioned problems with the common event study methodology might explain the mixed results coming from empirical M&A studies. Most studies agree that target firms can expect a positive average announcement return between 20 and 50 percent (e.g. Jarrell and Poulsen 1989; Chan et al. 2012; and Croci et al. 2012). Bidding firms pay these large premiums to incentivize target shareholders to tender their shares, conditional to a minimum number of shareholders agreeing to the deal. However, more recent literature finds that the premiums paid for targets vary significantly depending on bidder, target, and deal characteristics. For instance, a survey by Eckbo (2009) finds that the offer premium is higher in single-bid takeover contests than in multi-bid contests (consistent with preemptive bidding strategies). On the other hand, premiums are lower for toehold bidders (bidders acquiring a smaller stake in the target prior to the bid offer) and higher for public than for private bidders, as well as for targets with a higher level of managerial or institutional ownership (Bargeron et al. 2008). Additionally, because cash offers have direct tax implications for target shareholders, those offers should have higher premiums than stock-bids that allow capital gains to be deferred (Travlos 1987). Finally, Betton et al. (2008) find that the initial offer price rises by $0.80 if the target stock price increases by $1 during pre-bid run-ups, which usually occur as rumors about the takeover reach the market.

2.1.2.3 Bidding firms' announcement returns

Despite a large body of literature, evidence for bidding firms is much less conclusive. Roll (1986) theorizes that takeovers have no value for the shareholders of bidding firms. His managerial hubris hypothesis suggests that managers pay large premiums for targets (i.e. also firms with a known market price) because they commit positive valuation errors and "convince [themselves] that the market does not fully reflect the value of the combined firm" (Roll 1986, p. 199). As a consequence, premiums only represent wealth transfers from bidding to target shareholders and acquiring firms systematically overpay. This hypothesis is based on the same behavioral assumptions as the agency theory, according to which managers act in their own selfish interests, which can lead them to engage in value destroying activities (e.g. empire building). Overpayment may become even more severe when several competing bidders are involved. In such cases, "the winning bid [...], on average, overstate[s] the market's estimate of the expected takeover gain" and shareholders face negative average announcement returns of up to 14% (Varaiya and Ferris 1987, p. 64). The market also expects cross-industry takeovers (diversification) or acquisitions of growth firms to be primarily driven by managerial objectives. For these cases Morck et al. (1990) and Bhagat et al. (2005) find systematically lower bidder or combined bidder-target announcement returns.

Many empirical studies report "normal" (i.e. zero abnormal) announcement returns for bidding firms. This, however, might not have anything to do with the value gain expected from the takeover. Even if an acquisition promises a high positive net present value, the acquirer's share price might not be affected if the target is too small relative to that acquirer. Not surprisingly, Asquith et al. (1983) show that bidder's (absolute) announcement returns are positively related to the relative size of the target. Fuller et al. (2002) also point out that the stock price reaction to an announcement is only significant if that announcement comes as a surprise to the market: if a firm follows an active acquisition strategy, the market will only react to non-anticipated features of the deal. In these cases, not all information about the value of the takeover can be inferred from announcement returns. These facts make an objective empirical evaluation of tender offers more than difficult.

Empirical evidence for positive bidder announcement returns is scarce, but it exists. For instance, Asquith et al. (1983) show that average abnormal returns for bidding firms were small but significantly positive prior to the 1980s, ranging from 0.9% to 2.4% depending on the event window. Jarrell and Poulsen (1989) confirm this result but notice that returns were negative in the 1980s. More recent studies mostly observe negative abnormal returns for acquirers. For example, Andrade et al. (2001) report a range from –0.7% over a three-day event period to –3.8% over a longer window. Moeller et al. (2005) report positive equally weighted abnormal returns but show that shareholders lost 12 cents per dollar spent on acquisitions between 1998 and 2001, indicating a skewed distribution with a small number of "large loss" deals. Similarly, a working paper by Bayazitova et al. (2011) identifies so-called "mega-mergers," i.e. the top 1% of mergers with regard to deal value. These mergers are reported to have negative abnormal announcement returns of –3.2%, while all other deals have positive returns of about 1.5%. This finding is consistent with Roll's (1986) hubris theory: while the majority of deals is motivated by value-maximization, large M&A deals are likely to be driven by managerial interests and are therefore value-destroying.

These findings suggest that the deal size, the size of the target (relative to the acquirer), the number of competing bidders, the industry (degree of diversification), and managers tendency to hubris (possibly measured with corporate governance proxies) need to be taken into consideration in the analysis of takeover returns.

2.1.3 Disentangling synergistic gains and other informational effects

2.1.3.1 Information asymmetry and the method of payment

Why would firms engage in acquisitions if the expected return is zero or negative? Put differently, do mergers and acquisitions actually create value, e.g. by means of synergies? In order to answer this question, one needs to consider the managerial motives behind an acquisition. Outside shareholders have an informational disadvantage relative to managers and inside investors. In the mergers and acquisitions literature, this information asymmetry problem is not limited to managerial hubris but extends to the basic question of how a takeover should be financed. At first, this notion seems to contradict one of the basic corporate finance principles that the source of financing of an investment project is irrelevant as long as that project has a positive net present value. However, Travlos (1987) provides empirical evidence that the method of payment can indeed explain a significant fraction of the variation in M&A announcement returns. While offers made primarily in cash are associated with normal returns, stock offers are found to cause significant losses for the shareholders of the bidding firm. The reason for this discrepancy lies in the nature of a stock-financed acquisition. It is not just an investment project (as is the case with cash offers) but also a financing activity: the issuance of new equity. Since Myers and Majluf (1984), we know that if managers act in the interest of incumbent shareholders, they will try to take advantage of the prevalent informational asymmetry and only issue new equity if the "share of existing assets and slack going to new shareholders [is smaller or equal than] the increment to firm value obtained by old shareholders" (Myers and Majluf 1984, p. 199). According to the authors' equilibrium model, this is only the case if the firm's equity is overvalued. Hence, the model predicts that a seasoned equity offering (SEO) will tend to reduce the stock price in response to the overvaluation signal. This theoretical result is consistent with empirical evidence by Mikkelson and Partch (1986), among others, who find large decreases in share prices upon the announcement of common stock or convertible debt issues, as compared to the issuance of other securities.

The same rationale can be applied to the announcement of stock-financed acquisitions. Golubov et al. (2011) try to estimate the value effect of a takeover net of the hypothetical stock price drop associated with an equity issue. As it turns out, the average short-term CAR for stock-financed acquisitions of –2.56% is entirely due to the overvaluation signal (see section 2.1.3.2 for other negative revelation effects). The "pure" return of the takeover is found to be +0.1%, which is statistically indistinguishable from cash offer announcement returns. Hence, the financing-irrelevance principle also seems to hold for mergers and acquisitions. It could be argued that, despite this result, shareholders are worse off after the announcement of a stock-financed takeover and do not care about a hypothetical positive return. This argument, however, disregards the positive long-term effect of a value-adding acquisition. The equity's overvaluation will eventually be discovered even without the announcement of the takeover. On the other hand, long-term shareholders should benefit if the pure value of the takeover is considered positive. Savor and Lu (2009) provide empirical evidence for this notion. They show that stock-acquirers use takeovers to convert their overvalued equity into (less overvalued) hard assets and that successful stock-acquirers outperform failed ones by 13.6%, 22.2%, and 31.2% over a one-, two-, and three-year horizon, respectively. This result indicates that long-term shareholders indeed benefit from stock-financed acquisitions, despite negative announcement returns. Hansen (1987) provides a theory that directly relates a bidder's propensity to offer stock to the level of asymmetric information. Target shareholders will only tender their shares if the offer is higher than the actual value. The resulting adverse selection problem (high uncertainty about the target's asset value) can be avoided if stock is offered as payment. One implication of the model is that the probability of a stock bid increases with the relative size of the target. Croci et al. (2012) add to these findings by showing that targets receive higher premiums if bidders possess favorable asymmetric information about the target, i.e. if they perceive the "firm-specific risk regarding future synergies" as low. Under these circumstances, bidders are more inclined to offer cash, which the market interprets as evidence for the bidder having superior (positive) information about the target.

2.1.3.2 *Revelation, truncation, and information timing*

As is evident from the discussion above, M&A announcements carry information that is unrelated to the actual deal, making it difficult to determine its "true" incremental value for shareholders. In fact, it is plausible to assume that a takeover announcement always releases some negative information about the stand-alone value of a bidding firm. For example, it could indicate that a firm is no longer able to create profitable internal growth opportunities, e.g. due to a limited market size or a lack of resources, innovation, or organizational flexibility. This additional uncertainty about the future prospects of the firm, combined with the probability of managerial hubris and the rational revaluation of the firm after an implied equity issue, gives rise to the so-called "revelation" bias (cf. Bhagat et al. 2005, p. 4). In order to determine whether an acquisition itself is perceived as beneficial by shareholders, it is necessary to filter out revelation effects first.

A second bias that announcement returns suffer from is "truncation," which was discussed earlier. This bias is related to the success (or failure) probability of the announced acquisition. Since no deal is entirely certain to succeed (even less so without any post-announcement adjustments), the stock price reaction of both the bidder and the target will not reflect the full value effects of an ultimately successful transaction unless the event window is extended to the completion date, which introduces a great deal of noise (Bhagat et al. 2005).

A third noise factor is discussed by Masulis et al. (2011). There is a possibility that bidders time the announcement of a deal in order to smooth the stock price reaction. For example, managers tend to announce an acquisition together with "bad" news, e.g. unmet earnings targets, which artificially lowers the announcement returns. Also, bidders might "inflate" their stock price by releasing positive news prior to the deal announcement.

There are several recent studies that attempt to isolate synergistic gains from takeovers by disentangling value creation, revelation signals, and the truncation effect. In their pioneer paper, Bhagat et al. (2005) develop two techniques that address the aforementioned biases. First, the probability scaling model tackles the truncation bias by inflating the combined value improvement (both bidder and target) with the sum of the (ex-post) probability that the first bidder succeeds and the probability that a later bid does. The second approach, the intervention method, allows inferring takeover value improvements from stock returns associated with intervening events such as competing bids. These bids decrease the probability that the first bidder will succeed in acquiring the target. Thus, if the stock reacts negatively to a competing bid, the expected value improvement is larger than the purchase price; if the stock reacts positively, the transaction is expected to be value destroying. Additionally, the method accounts for the chance of a price increase upon arrival of a competing bid (cf. Bhagat et al. 2005). The authors find that the combined value improvements, net of revelation and truncation bias, amount to about 13%, indicating that these acquisitions do create value.

In a similar manner, Masulis et al. (2011) examine takeover bids that failed for exogenous reasons. They find a 25.5% combined value gain for bidders and targets, and show that successful bidders significantly outperform failed bidders after consummation/failure. In her analysis of withdrawn and completed mergers, Risik (2010) argues that, when a merger is withdrawn, returns associated with the merger should reverse while those related to revelation should not. She reports that completed acquirers outperform withdrawn ones by 12.3% over the six months after the announcement.

To conclude this first part of the literature review on M&A related corporate finance, we can summarize as follows. Mergers occur in waves that seem to be triggered by exogenous shocks such as deregulation or technological innovations. While target shareholders receive a substantial premium upon announcement of a takeover, shareholders of bidding firms have either normal or negative abnormal returns. Especially stock-financed acquisitions were long considered to be value-destroying. However, there is evidence that most M&A transactions have positive wealth effects for bidding firms, regardless of the method of payment. Since announcement returns suffer from revelation and truncation biases, these positive value effects do not become immediately apparent. In order to isolate the incremental value from mergers and acquisitions, announcement returns need to be adjusted to account for the implied revaluation of the bidder's stand-alone value as well as for the probability that the deal might fail.

2.2 Cross-section of options and stocks: Evidence from M&A transactions

The second part of this literature review covers theoretical and empirical evidence related to options and their predictive power for stock returns. Following an introduction on the basic principles of option trading, the first subsection examines the lead-lag relationship between options and equity markets. Since both markets are closely tied to one another, the following questions arise: How much of a firm's stock price is actually determined in the forward-looking options market? If there are informed traders, in which market do they trade (first)? Accordingly, can option prices or other related variables predict stock prices? And if this is the case, how long does this predictive power persist? The second subsection builds upon the first, narrowing these questions down to corporate events. This part will also close the circle and return to the theme of M&A transactions, providing evidence on the question whether takeover announcements, abnormal returns, and (both short- and long-term) wealth effects can be predicted by informed option trading proxies.

2.2.1 Price discovery process in the options and stock market

2.2.1.1 Definitions

According to basic financial theory, an option is a redundant security whose price is derived from an "underlying," i.e. from a primary instrument such as a stock. Nevertheless, options can also be written on commodities, futures, and basically all assets that have an observable market price. In terms of stock options, redundancy means that every option can be replicated by a combination of the underlying stock and a risk-free bond. This holds, however, only in complete markets without transaction costs, taxes, arbitrage opportunities, and short selling constraints. The well-known and widely used option pricing model by Black and Scholes (1973) and Merton (1973) (henceforth BSM) builds upon these assumptions and derives the option price from the stock price, the strike price, the risk-free rate, the option's maturity, and the stock volatility that is expected over the life of the option. While the buyer of a call option has the right (but not the obligation) to buy a certain amount of the underlying for the strike price from the seller ("writer"), a put option entitles the holder to sell the underlying at the strike price. The contract between the buyer and the seller specifies whether the option can be exercised at any time prior to the expiration date ("American" option) or only on the day of expiration ("European" option). The BSM formula can only be applied to European calls and puts on non-dividend paying stocks. Most traded options are, however, American and need to be valued by means of other models, e.g. binomial trees.

In reality, options cannot be perfectly replicated because of transaction costs and the indivisibility of common stocks. Additionally, traders with negative private information often have no choice but to trade options in lieu of stock due to short selling constraints in the stock market. Option prices are determined by the trading activity in both stock and options markets. The large trading volumes that can be observed in the market indicate that investors take on substantial positions in derivatives. It can therefore be concluded that options are in fact non-redundant securities that are value-adding to at least some market participants.

2.2.1.2 The role of informed traders

Since Black (1975) argued that the leverage in options could incentivize traders with private information to trade in options markets, an ever-increasing body of literature has tried to determine the role that options play in the price discovery process of stocks. In theory, new information disseminating into the marketplace should be incorporated in stock and options markets simultaneously. Yet because of market inefficiencies, this need not always be the case. Some early research in this area has revealed little evidence that options markets are particularly attractive to informed traders. For example, Vijh (1990) argues that while the implied leverage in options might attract some informed traders, this is equally true for noise traders (i.e. speculators). He measures the extent of information-related trading, using the adverse-selection component of the option's bid-ask spread (premium charged by dealers to cover losses from trades against better-informed traders) as a proxy, and finds evidence against active information trading. Stephan and Whaley (1990) compare stock price changes implied from option prices with actual stock price changes and conclude that stock markets reflect new information fifteen to twenty minutes earlier than options markets. Chan et al. (2002) focus on the net-trade volume of options and stocks and its effect on quote revisions. The net-trade volume refers to a temporary order imbalance, or more specifically, to the difference between buyer- and seller-initiated trading volumes. While option net-trade volume does not seem to have any predictive ability, stock net-trade carries information about both stock and option quote revisions.

Nevertheless, there is substantial evidence to the contrary, namely that options markets can lead stock markets. Using their sequential trade model, Easley et al. (1998) investigate the role of option trading volume in the price discovery process. Consistent with Vijh (1990), they find no evidence that call or put option volumes predict stock prices. However, when they aggregate "positive news" option volumes (i.e. trades entered into by traders informed of good news, e.g. buying a call or selling a put) and "negative news" volumes (i.e. trading on bad news, e.g. buying a put or selling a call), the authors show that these aggregate volumes do in fact carry information about future stock returns, and that options markets lead stock markets by about twenty to thirty minutes (Easley et al. 1998). Pan and Poteshman (2006) apply an approach similar to Chan et al. (2002), using call and put option volumes that are initiated by buyers to open new positions. These volumes are not publicly observable. They form stock portfolios based on put-call ratios and find that the quintile portfolio with the lowest put-call ratio outperforms the one with the highest put-call ratio by over 40bps per day or 1% per week. In comparison, publicly observable signals do not seem to have predictive power. The authors conclude that the economic source of their result is the "valuable private information in the option volume rather than an inefficiency across the stock and option market" (Pan and Poteshman 2006, p. 873). Chakravarty et al. (2004) show that informed traders trade in both stock and options markets, and estimate the option market's contribution to price discovery at about 17%. More information can be derived from options if option liquidity is high (i.e. trading volume is high, spreads are narrow) relative to stock liquidity, and if implied leverage is high. Finally, Ni et al. (2008) note that options are the preferred instruments of traders with information about future volatility (but not about the directional movement). Arguing that vega (measure for an option's exposure to volatility) is positive for both calls and puts, they construct a measure for volatility demand by treating the buy volume for calls and puts as positive demand and the sell volume as negative demand. The net volatility demand is found to predict future realized stock volatility, showing that there are informed volatility traders in the market. This effect is persistent over one week.

2.2.1.3 THE PREDICTIVE POWER OF OPTION IMPLIED VOLATILITIES

While most of the early research on the predictive power of options uses option prices and volumes, a relatively new strand of literature is concerned with more implicit option trading proxies such as option implied volatility. The implied volatility of an option (henceforth IV) is the market's expectation of the future volatility of the underlying over the life of the option. IV is not directly observable but can be inferred from an option pricing model like BSM by using the observed market price and solving iteratively for volatility. Ceteris paribus, high IV options are more expensive than low IV options.

Cremers and Weinbaum (2010) show that the difference between implied volatilities of call and put options on the same underlying equity, with the same strike price and with the same maturity can be used to identify price pressures and predict stock returns in the cross-section. Amin et al. (2004) call this difference the *implied volatility spread* (henceforth IV spread). IV spreads are deviations from the put-call-parity but do not usually represent arbitrage opportunities, which is due to the fact that the put-call-parity is an inequality for American options (cf. Hull 2012) and does not account for transaction costs. Along the lines of the sequential trade model of Easley et al. (1998), Cremers and Weinbaum (2010) argue that the presence of informed investors in the options market results in option price deviations from put-call parity in the direction of the private information. It can therefore be expected that a higher call-put IV spread is indicative of positive news not yet reflected in the stock price. In fact, the authors find a positive relation between IV spread and future stock returns. A portfolio that is long in stocks with relatively expensive calls and short in stocks with relatively expensive puts earns an abnormal return of about 50bps per week. This effect is stronger when option liquidity is high and stock liquidity is low, which is consistent with the findings of Chakravarty et al. (2004). Notably, the authors control not only for the four Fama and French (1993) and Carhart (1997) factors but also for systematic return skewness, as suggested by Harvey and Siddique (2000). They justify this additional factor with the concern that stocks with high call (put) prices might have positively (negatively) skewed return distributions to begin with. Bali and Hovakimian (2009) also provide evidence for a positive relation between IV spread and future returns. In their analysis, IV spread proxies for stock price *jump risk,* which commands a risk premium. In addition, they theorize that the difference between the (one-month) lagged realized volatility and implied volatility proxies for *volatility risk.* The authors find this second spread to be negatively related to future returns. Bollerslev et al. (2009) basically come to the same conclusion. They show that the difference between (model-free) implied and realized variances positively predicts stock market returns, especially over quarterly horizons.

Another recently introduced proxy for informed option trading is *implied volatility skewness* (henceforth IV skew). Xing et al. (2010) define IV skew as the difference between the implied volatilities of out-of-the-money (OTM) put options and at-the-money (ATM) call options on the same underlying and with the same expiration date. OTM puts usually trade at a risk premium relative to ATM options because investors have an aversion toward negative jumps in stock prices and overestimate the probability of downward movements. This common characteristic of stock options is also known as the volatility smirk or smile. If some investors have unfavorable private information, they will buy (cheap) OTM puts. As a result, these puts become relatively expensive, which steepens the IV smirk (Xing et al. 2010). Xing et al. find evidence that IV skew is negatively related to future stock returns, i.e. stocks exhibiting the steepest smirks underperform those with the least pronounced smirks by 21bps per week. The effect is persistent over about six months. The persistency found in the empirical literature suggests inefficiencies in the stock market that cannot instantaneously incorporate the information provided in the options market. Alternatively, it could be argued that it is not the stock market's inefficiency that drives these results but rather a misperception of the importance of the options market in the price discovery process. If the IV smirk is not regarded as a gauge of informed trading but as a measure of common investor sentiment (overly pessimistic investors buy insurance in light of increasing trading activity and volatility), stock prices will only adjust very slowly.

Doran et al. (2007) point out that option pricing models that aim to improve the model-fit over the BSM (which assumes constant volatility) need to account for the volatility smirk and incorporate a jump risk premium. For example, Bakshi et al. (1997) show that the inclusion of stock price jumps improves the performance of their stochastic volatility model, especially for the pricing of short-term options. According to Todorov (2010), the premium investors require for taking variance risk (particularly jump risk) varies over time and increases immediately after the occurrence of a price jump. This shows that extreme price movements drive the risk aversion of market participants, i.e. risk aversion is time-varying. A more detailed review of other option pricing models that include volatility and jump risk is beyond the scope of this paper. Yan (2011) provides a comprehensive survey of the most relevant works in this field. Nevertheless, the finding that both IV spread and IV skew seem to proxy for jump risk make these factors particularly intriguing with regard to event studies that explore the predictability of corporate announcements, that are expected to cause large price jumps for involved firms. The last subsection of this review will therefore focus on these announcements, especially mergers and acquisitions.

2.2.2 Event studies: predicting announcement returns with option trading proxies

2.2.2.1 Trading activity around corporate announcements (earnings)

If option markets are indeed venues for traders with superior information, then perhaps option characteristics such as prices, volumes, or implied volatilities can be used to predict the direction of stock prices after such announcements. Donders et al. (2000) assume that investors place delta and vega bets in anticipation of corporate news. As a consequence, open interest, option prices, and implied volatilities rise just before earnings announcements and drop again after the information is revealed. Amin and Lee (1997) find that option trading volume increases by 10 to 15 percent in the four days prior to earnings announcements while the stock market does not show signs of abnormal trading activity. Consistent with this result, Roll et al. (2010) show that the daily options/stocks trading volume ratio (O/S) rises significantly before such announcements. This elevated trading activity prior to earnings announcements suggests a liquidity surge in the options market relative to the stock market. As discussed earlier, this can be associated with a higher predictive power of trading proxies such as IV spread and IV skew. In fact, most studies come to the conclusion that options markets only play an important role in the price discovery if "extreme informational events" such as corporate announcements are pending and that they are not very informative in normal times (e.g. Cao et al. 2005).

With regard to earnings announcements and in line with the above results, Driessen et al. (2012) find that higher IV spreads are associated with good news, resulting not only in higher future stock returns but also in higher unexpected earnings and more positive analyst recommendations/forecast changes. The reverse is true for IV skew. The authors conclude that the predictive power of IV spread/skew on news-days is twice as large as on non-news-days. Roll et al. (2010) provide evidence for a positive relation between the pre-earnings announcement O/S ratio and post-announcement *absolute* cumulative abnormal returns. Without separating positive and negative news trades (cf. Easley et al. 1998), the O/S ratio can certainly not predict whether the earnings surprise will be positive or negative, but it seems to be a good indication of the magnitude of the reaction. Chesney et al. (2012) add to this research by analyzing individual trade characteristics instead of aggregates. They filter for trades with large increments in open interest to identify option informed trading and find that future returns are almost monotonically increasing with the size of these increments. The authors' results indicate that informed trading clusters around certain corporate events, both scheduled (quarterly earnings) and unscheduled (M&A or even the 9/11 terrorist attacks). Additionally, most of the detected trades are positions in puts rather than in calls.

2.2.2.2 Predictability of M&A announcement returns

Jayamaran et al. (1991) were among the first to test whether the options market can anticipate M&A deals. They reason that call option prices depend on the expected variance of future stock returns and that, because variance increases when new information is disseminated into the market, options should reflect this information if the market anticipates a takeover bid. They show that implied volatilities of target firms indeed rise significantly prior to a first bid. Cao et al. (2005) point out that, as opposed to earnings announcements, takeover announcements are not prescheduled. Consequently, a surge in pre-announcement option trading is even more likely to be initiated by traders acting on private information than by speculators. This should further increase the predictability of stock returns by these trading activities. In fact, Cao et al. discover that generally uninformative call volume imbalances (buyer- minus seller-initiated call volume, scaled by the volume during a benchmark period) of target firms become highly predictive of next-day returns before M&A announcements. Since lagged stock imbalances do not seem to have this kind of significant predictive power, Cao et al. conclude that the options market displaces the stock market as the primary venue for informed traders around M&A announcements. Post-announcement volume imbalances do not carry information about the ultimate outcome of the transaction. Furthermore, short-term OTM calls are found to have the largest volume imbalances, i.e. the highest predictability.

Chan et al. (2012) focus on bidding firms and provide evidence that strong inferences can be drawn from option IV spread/skew about M&A announcement returns, i.e. positive (negative) abnormal returns can be expected if pre-announcement option IV spread is high (low) and IV skew is low (high). Again, results are more pronounced for bidders whose options are relatively liquid compared to the underlying stock. Here, option liquidity is measured by the daily average bid-ask spread; stock liquidity is calculated using the Amihud's (2002) ILLIQ ratio (absolute stock return divided by trading volume). A calendar-time portfolio regression reveals that IV skew also seems to have significant post-announcement, long-run performance predictability. Furthermore, Chan et al. (2012) validate the results by Roll et al. (2010) for M&A cases, showing that the options/stocks (O/S) trading volume ratio is positively related to absolute bidder announcement returns. Finally, the authors assert that IV spread/skew also possess some predictive power for the returns of a small sample of target firms.

Wang (2009) investigates implied volatilities *after* an announcement to draw inferences about the market's perception of the deal's success probability. For cash bids, he constructs a volatility ratio that compares the target's observed IV with a "fallback" IV (historical average) and shows that this ratio converges towards 1 for ultimately failed transactions but not for successful ones. This finding shows that despite a drop in trading volume and liquidity, implied volatilities can still carry relevant information after the announcement. It might also be an indication that option trading proxies have predictive power with regard to the final outcome of a takeover. Martinez et al. (2009) develop an option pricing formula from which both the (risk-neutral) success probability of the deal and the target's fallback price can be derived. The estimated success probability is shown to be a better predictor of the deal outcome than the commonly used "naive" method, which evaluates the proximity of the current stock price to the offer price relative to the pre-announcement price. The method could prove useful to assess the offer premium and work out the truncation dilemma discussed in section 2.1.3.2.

The second part of this literature review on the cross-section of options and stocks can be summarized as follows. The value of an option is formally tied to the price of its underlying. In imperfect markets, however, this relation is not as strict as theory suggests; and one can expect either the stock market or the options market to lag behind until new information has disseminated into both markets. Empirical evidence shows that some informed option trading proxies such as volume imbalances, open interest, net volatility demand, the relative option-stock (O/S) trading volume, and implied volatilities have predictive power for future stock price movements. More recent literature attributes significant predictability to the (call-put) implied volatility spread and the slope of the implied volatility smirk. This predictability is often attributed to the presence of informed traders, and it seems to depend heavily on option liquidity. This liquidity is highest around corporate events such as quarterly earnings or M&A announcements, which is why most studies conclude that options markets only add to the price discovery process around these events. With regard to mergers and acquisitions, research finds that some of the aforementioned proxies can predict the direction and potentially the strength of the market reaction on the announcement day and, to a certain extent, even the outcome of the transaction.

2.3 Conceptual framework and hypothesis development

Looking at the combined research in both the corporate finance literature and the M&A-related literature on the cross-section of options and stocks, two observations stand out: Firstly, most studies focus on bidding firms and neglect the smaller number of listed target firms. This phenomenon can be explained by the fact that targets are often not publicly listed and usually do not have options traded on their stock. As a result, the number of sample deals is reduced tremendously which also reduces the statistical significance of the results. The sample is further downsized because both stocks and options of target firms are usually not very liquid securities. Also, the literature prefers bidding firms because bidder announcement returns can help to understand whether takeovers are value-creating. Secondly, empirical evidence suggesting that certain bidder, target, and deal characteristics have an effect on M&A announcement returns is widely ignored by the asset pricing side of the literature. For example, takeover premiums are found to be related to the method of payment (e.g. Travlos 1987), the number of bids (e.g. Eckbo 2009), the pre-announcement price run-up (e.g. Betton et al. 2008), the type of bidder (i.e. public or private), and the target's ownership structure (Bargeron et al. 2008).

If some traders have private information about a future takeover, and if they trade on this privileged information in the options market, pre-announcement option demand should have predictive power for announcement returns. Chan et al. (2012) provide evidence supporting this hypothesis for acquirer firms by using implied volatility (IV) spread, IV skew, and the option-to-stock volume ratio (O/S) as proxies for "informed option trading". Target firms might be even more attractive to informed traders because of the high takeover premiums paid to target shareholders. If this is the case, target and deal characteristics could help us to learn more about the nature of informed (option) trading. What kind of information do traders have about the target? How accurate is this information? For instance, do they know about the financing details of the offer? And if they have private information about an upcoming takeover, do traders purchase options or stocks? These questions have not been addressed in the previous literature. If the predictive power of the aforementioned informed option trading proxies depends on certain deal characteristics that should only be known to firm insiders, this could point towards illegal insider trading. In this case, regulators might need to increase their monitoring efforts.

Combining informed option trading theory with deal characteristics that have been shown to affect takeover premiums can contribute to our understanding of "informed trading" and the price discovery in financial markets. This study will thus attempt to close the existing gap in the literature by answering the following research question:

What information do "informed" option traders have with regard to the target firm and deal before the official takeover announcement?

To answer this question, a sufficiently large sample of target firms with liquid options is required. Research on bidding firms has shown that trading volume increases and bid-ask spreads decrease around announcements corporate events. A surge in trading activity before unscheduled takeover announcements points toward the presence of traders with private information. It can be assumed that these traders not only trade in the stocks of bidding firms but also in target stocks and options. If this is the case, the liquidity of these securities might be sufficiently high to overcome the traditional problems faced by asset pricing studies with regard to small firms. The first hypothesis is therefore as follows:

H1: Takeover announcements are preceded by abnormal liquidity in options of target firms.

Abnormal trading activity only shows that traders believe to have information about an upcoming event. It does not reveal what kind of information these traders really have. Abnormal liquidity could simply be driven by market rumors. To assess whether traders are truly informed, it is necessary to identify informed option trading proxies that have predictive power for future market movements. In the case of target firms, they should predict the takeover premium. The literature suggests three such proxies: IV spread, IV skew, and O/S. The second hypothesis examines this relationship:

H2: Implied volatility spread, implied volatility skew, and the O/S ratio have predictive power for the size of the takeover premium.

Assuming that there is informed option trading prior to the announcement, the nature of the information is still uncertain. Traders could have information about the method of payment, i.e. whether the deal is mainly financed with cash or with new equity. In this context, most studies focus on the overvalued-equity hypothesis by Myers and Majluf (1984), which predicts lower acquirer returns if stock is issued. With regard to target firms, Travlos (1987) stresses the tax advantages of stock bids for target shareholders and the resulting higher required premium for cash bids. Croci et al. (2012) show that a cash bid signals favorable news to investors about the value of firm. If informed traders know about the financing of the deal, this information should be reflected in the relationship between any of the informed option trading proxies and the takeover premium.

H3: Informed traders have information about the method of payment, i.e. whether the deal will be primarily financed with cash or with stock.

In addition, the question arises whether a trader's information is based on facts or speculation. An instrument that might help to answer this question is managerial entrenchment, or control (e.g. by means of managerial stock ownership). Stulz (1988) finds that higher ownership decreases the chance of a successful tender offer, but increases the takeover premium if an offer is made. If informed traders know for certain that an offer will be made, entrenchment might prompt them to increase pre-announcement option trading because of the higher expected premium. By contrast, if the information is speculative, entrenchment could diminish the number of informed option trades as there is a lower probability that a bid will be made in the first place.

H4: More managerial entrenchment encourages traders with accurate information to make informed option trades but discourages those who act upon speculation.

Finally, industry insiders and financial analysts with a focus on a particular industry could have an informational advantage over other investors if both the target and the bidder have their core business in the same industry. This argument motivates the last hypothesis:

H5: Options have a higher predictability for takeover premiums if the target and bidder are in the same industry.

3. Data and Methodology

3.1 Data

Sample size is one of the most critical factors in the analysis of target firms. As mentioned before, target firms are often not publicly listed and are less likely to have liquid options traded on their stocks. In line with earlier research, I use OptionMetrics Ivy database to obtain daily option data, including closing bid and ask prices, expiration date, strike price, volume, open interest, and implied volatilities. According to OptionMetrics, these volatilities already account for the option type (European or American) and discrete dividend payments. Option data is available for U.S. firms only, starting in January 1996. As a consequence, my sample only consists of takeovers that were announced between February 1996 and December 2012. January 1996 was excluded because some explanatory variables require option data to be available up to one month prior to the announcement. I identified all merger and acquisition announcements by means of the Securities Data Company Platinum database (SDC), filtering target firms by location (U.S.) and target public status (public). Furthermore, I only included deals in which the acquirer was seeking to own more than 50% of the target after the transaction. SDC also provides data on deal characteristics such as deal success, attitude (i.e. hostile), mode of payment, and target/acquirer industry (4-digit SIC). The resulting initial sample consisted of 11,499 deals or 9,752 individual firms.

Using the CUSIP identifiers of these firms, I obtained daily option data from OptionMetrics (via the Wharton Research Data Services, WRDS). In the request form, I limited the search to options with maturities between 10 and 60 days to exclude the most illiquid options. This is consistent with Xing et al. (2010). In total, I retrieved option data for 2,893 bids or 2,253 target firms. For these firms, I also obtained stock prices (opening and closing), stock trading volumes, and holding period returns from CRSP database (Center for Research in Security Prices). Only those deals for which I had at least 205 days of daily stock price data before the announcement were included in the final sample. In case a target firm received more than one bid, subsequent bids were only included in the sample if the estimation window did not overlap with the event window of the previous bid. Following this procedure, the final sample consists of 2,390 observations including 2,129 individual firms.

In addition to option and stock data, I gathered earnings announcement dates from Institutional Brokers' Estimate System (I/B/E/S) and yearly data on the targets' corporate governance (e.g. CEO tenure, board composition, managerial ownership) from WRDS' Corporate Library datasets. The latter information is only available for the years 2001 to 2011, or a total of 903 announcements. Finally, I added accounting information for each target from COMPUSTAT, in particular the book value of equity, the net income, and the revenues (all quarterly).

3.2 METHODOLOGY AND SUMMARY STATISTICS

3.2.1 CUMULATIVE ABNORMAL RETURNS

In order to assess whether or not some market participants with private information trade in target options before a takeover announcement, I follow the existing literature and conduct a standard event study with each firm's cumulative abnormal returns (CARs) around the takeover announcement as the dependent variable. The mechanics of this methodology were already discussed in section 2.1.2.1. This section specifies the parameters of the benchmark model and elaborates on the length of the estimation and event windows.

Following Chan et al. (2012), CARs are cumulated over day t and $t+1$, where t is defined as the announcement day. This event period is unusually short compared to other studies, but it can be justified because the market reaction to the bid will instantaneously reflect the offer premium. Extending the window would only add unnecessary noise and would not significantly contribute to overcoming the truncation bias. In addition, the three option trading proxies are calculated for day *t–1* or over the five days preceding the announcement. Adding day *t–1* or any previous day to the event window would therefore bias the results. The estimation period covers exactly 200 trading days and ends on day *t–6*. The five days prior to the event are excluded because informed traders will also trade in stocks. Including them in the estimation window would upward bias the expected returns and decrease the CARs. If the announcement day happens to fall on a non-trading day, the announcement date reported by SDC is replaced by the following trading day. Finally, an announcement is excluded from the sample if a prior bid lies in that announcement's benchmark period, i.e. in a series of bids within a short period of time only the first announcement is included. This method assures that the relation between the option trading proxies and the CARs is in fact driven by traders with private information and not by the market reaction to prior bids.

I use the Carhart four-factor model as the benchmark model. Cremers and Weinbaum (2010) point out that their IV spread specification (see below) might be problematic if the IVs are systematically related to skewness in the underlying return distribution. To control for idiosyncratic skewness risk, they add a coskewness factor to the benchmark model, following Harvey and Siddique (2000). Driessen et al. (2012) and Chan et al. (2012) do not account for this risk factor. Due to time limitations, I will also refrain from including it in the pricing model. To address Cremers and Weinbaum's concern, I will instead include a control variable for pre-announcement stock return skewness in my main regressions. Thus, the benchmark model for the estimation of expected returns is specified as follows:

$$R_{i,t} - Rf_t = \alpha_i + \beta_{1,i}MKT_t + \beta_{2,i}SMB_t + \beta_{3,i}HML_t + \beta_{4,i}MOM_t + \varepsilon_{i,t}\,, \tag{1}$$

where Rf_t is the risk-free rate, *MKT* is the market risk premium, and *SMB*, *HML*, and *MOM* refer to the long-short portfolios that capture the size, book-to-market, and momentum effect, respectively. I downloaded these factors and the daily risk-free rate (corresponds to the one-month U.S. Treasury bill rate) from the Fama-French dataset on WRDS.[1] $R_{i,t}$ is the holding period return (adjusted for stock splits and dividend payments) from CRSP. CARs are derived by summing the abnormal returns on each day τ during the event window, with $R^* - Rf$ being the excess holding period return on day τ.

$$CAR_{i,\tau} = \sum_{\tau=0}^{\tau=1} \left(R^*_{i,\tau} - Rf_\tau\right) - \hat{\alpha}_i - \hat{\beta}_{1,i}MKT_\tau - \hat{\beta}_{2,i}SMB_\tau - \hat{\beta}_{3,i}HML_\tau - \hat{\beta}_{4,i}MOM_\tau \tag{2}$$

[1] The source of this data is Ken French's website: http://mba.tuck.dartmouth.edu/pages/faculty/ken.french/index.html

Table 1 reports the summary statistics for average two-day CARs. Based on the *[t, t+1]* event window, we observe a mean CAR of 17.2% for the final sample with a standard deviation of 24.1%. The median is only 13.5%, and the distribution is positively skewed. The average t-statistics suggest that the mean CARs are significantly positive. However, a look at the raw data reveals that about one-third of the individual CARs are not statistically significant at conventional levels. This may come as a surprise since one would expect the CARs to reflect the offer premiums, which should be highly positive. But looking at the first quartile of the distribution, and the minimum in particular, I find that there are indeed firms that have highly negative CARs of up to –92%. This minimum CAR was the result of a dissolution announcement by 3Dfx Interactive Inc. at the end of 2000, which was sold to Nvidia Corp. on the same day. This example shows that financial or economic distress can have tremendous adverse effects on the offer price. In general, Table 1 shows that the number of takeovers fluctuates over the years, ranging from 62 in 2002 to 247 in 1999. The mean CAR varies between 12.5% and 23.8%. The number of takeovers follows the overall economic conditions, with most takeovers occurring during the dotcom bubble and before the dawn of the subprime crisis. It does not seem that the mean CARs follow a similar pattern.

TABLE 1: SUMMARY STATISTICS FOR TARGET CARS

This table presents summary statistics for the cumulative abnormal announcement returns (CARs) of U.S. takeover targets. The CARs are computed for an event window from *t* to *t+1* with an estimation period of *t-205* to *t-6*, using a Carhart 4-factor model (alternative measures are presented in Appendix 1). N represents the number of announcements per year. MEAN is the equal-weighted CAR, SD is the standard deviation, and SKEW is the abnormal return skewness. t-statistics were computed by aggregating the mean standard errors resulting from regression (1) over the two event days and the respective firms. MIN, Q1, MEDIAN, Q3, and MAX represent the minimum, 1st quartile, median, 3rd quartile, and maximum of the distribution, respectively.

YEAR	N	MEAN	SD	t-STAT	SKEW	MIN	Q1	MEDIAN	Q3	MAX
1996	120	13.31%	15.99%	5.96	0.33	-31.92%	2.40%	12.29%	23.01%	61.27%
1997	146	12.81%	18.58%	6.63	0.55	-46.56%	0.43%	11.12%	22.05%	82.49%
1998	227	12.91%	18.89%	7.91	0.97	-35.61%	-0.07%	10.78%	22.95%	88.60%
1999	247	15.71%	20.24%	8.81	1.52	-29.83%	2.84%	12.06%	26.65%	143.70%
2000	212	16.62%	25.39%	8.33	0.27	-92.09%	1.55%	13.01%	30.46%	104.65%
2001	119	20.11%	31.61%	6.63	2.19	-63.87%	2.68%	14.00%	31.76%	207.28%
2002	62	12.46%	24.58%	3.27	0.98	-60.00%	1.10%	11.00%	22.22%	113.05%
2003	73	20.50%	34.27%	6.94	4.72	-11.07%	4.29%	11.77%	24.15%	256.96%
2004	89	13.26%	14.22%	5.68	0.61	-12.35%	1.25%	12.64%	20.78%	59.21%
2005	118	15.46%	18.25%	8.10	0.86	-28.41%	3.14%	13.40%	24.05%	77.22%
2006	160	15.30%	14.43%	9.64	1.51	-6.32%	5.44%	12.13%	22.03%	93.44%
2007	193	17.72%	21.11%	12.21	2.74	-66.34%	6.63%	14.57%	23.59%	161.95%
2008	124	23.75%	40.96%	10.29	3.23	-68.06%	3.80%	16.23%	33.23%	322.27%
2009	107	21.26%	34.21%	6.97	3.09	-66.39%	4.74%	15.57%	28.09%	247.46%
2010	118	22.01%	21.44%	11.00	0.68	-43.50%	5.56%	19.03%	35.56%	95.77%
2011	146	21.18%	24.25%	12.43	1.22	-66.92%	3.84%	17.35%	31.97%	140.31%
2012	129	22.60%	23.75%	11.16	1.38	-28.39%	5.51%	20.12%	34.46%	138.30%
All	**2,390**	**17.22%**	**24.08%**	**33.55**	**2.63**	**-92.09%**	**2.96%**	**13.48%**	**26.88%**	**322.27%**

In Appendix 1, I report three alternative takeover premium measures. The first one extends the event window to include day *t–1*, resulting in a slightly higher mean CAR of 18.5% and a standard deviation of 24.5% (see Panel A). Because of informed trading in the stock market before the official announcement, this CAR is expected to be higher on average. The second measure in Panel B is the average CAR based on open-to-close returns. For these abnormal returns, I also used equation (2), but instead of using holding period returns I calculated open-to-close returns with opening prices obtained from CRSP. The idea behind this decision was to address the non-synchronicity problem suggested by Battalio and Schultz (2006): U.S. option markets close two minutes later than stock markets, which means that option closing prices have an informational advantage. Ignoring this fact might lead to biased conclusions about the predictive abilities of option data for stock returns. Some papers circumvent this issue by using next-day open-to-close returns. However, the summary statistics show that the mean open-to-close CARs are much lower and also insignificant. This might be an indication that most announcements are made before the exchange opens. It is not reasonable to assume that the announcement occurred within the two minutes after the closing of the markets on the previous day, because this would also change the announcement date reported by SDC. Therefore, I am confident that my results are not affected by the non-synchronicity problem. The third measure in Panel C is not CAR but the actual offer premium. This is the ratio of the offer price to the target's stock price one week prior to the bid (minus 1). The ratio was obtained from SDC as well. The summary statistics show that the average offer premium is about 33.7%, which is almost twice as high as the mean CAR in Table 1. This can be explained by the stock price run-up before the announcement as well as by the truncation bias discussed earlier, which are not reflected in CARs. Also, the standard deviation is much higher. Due to my model setup (explanatory variables are measured on day *t–1*), I cannot use either of those alternative variables in my main analysis. However, they do offer additional information about the announcement of takeover bids which is why they are included in the appendix.

3.2.2 Primary explanatory variables

The relevant variables were already briefly discussed in the literature review. In this section, I define them more formally and mention the filters and restrictions I applied. Cremers and Weinbaum (2010) and Xing et al. (2010) introduce two of the more promising option trading proxies that seem to have predictive power for takeover announcement returns: implied volatility spread and implied volatility skew. I follow these papers to construct both measures. The implied volatility spread is defined as the average of differences in implied volatilities (*IV*) between call and put options with the same strike price and expiration date:

$$IVspread_{i.t} = \sum_{j=1}^{n_{i,t}} w_{j,t}^{i} \left(IV_{j,t}^{i,call} - IV_{j,t}^{i,put}\right), \quad (3)$$

where i refers to the firm and j to the call-put pair. Matched put-call pairs were weighted by the sum of open interest in the call and the put (w) to account for liquidity issues of deep ITM/OTM options. Following Cremers and Weinbaum, I excluded option pairs for which either the call or the put had zero open interest or a bid price of zero, or if the implied volatilities were not reported in OptionMetrics. For pairs with more than one put or call, I removed those options that had an IV above 200% (see Xing et al., 2010). For the remaining cases, I matched those pairs for which the IVs were closest to one another, because in theory matched puts and calls should have the same IV. This method was only applied to a small fraction of pairs and mismatches should therefore not affect the overall results. As an alternative measure, I calculated the $IV\ spread_{ATM}$ that only includes ATM option pairs, i.e. pairs for which the strike price is closest to the closing stock price. I calculate this measure because the predictive ability of IV spreads that include OTM/ITM options could be directly related to the IV skew (see below) instead of to the spread itself. To calculate the options' moneyness, I matched the daily option data with the underlying stock prices and calculated the strike-to-stock price ratios.

TABLE 2: SUMMARY STATISTICS IMPLIED VOLATILITY SPREAD

This table summarizes the implied volatility spreads (IV spread) for day *t-1*, i.e. only for the day before the takeover announcement. In Panel A, IV spread is calculated as the difference in implied volatilities between call and put options with the same strike price and expiration date. Daily IV spreads are aggregated over all put-call pairs traded on a particular day and weighted by open interest. N is the number of events. MEAN represents the arithmetic average (equal-weighted) of all IV spreads. Panel B shows IV spreads which only include at-the-money calls and puts, i.e. options with a strike-to-stock price ratio closest to 1.

Panel A: Open-interest weighted IV Spread										**Panel B: IV Spread, ATM**		
YEAR	N	MEAN	SD	SKEW	MIN	Q1	MEDIAN	Q3	MAX	N	MEAN	SD
1996	68	0.0146	0.1111	0.00	-0.3650	-0.0254	0.0093	0.0719	0.4691	68	0.0150	0.1114
1997	107	0.0165	0.0987	0.30	-0.2997	-0.0350	0.0139	0.0550	0.3422	107	0.0225	0.1008
1998	170	0.0100	0.1012	-0.74	-0.6208	-0.0247	0.0062	0.0451	0.3862	170	0.0144	0.0949
1999	185	0.0254	0.0974	-0.45	-0.4509	-0.0220	0.0189	0.0781	0.3898	185	0.0203	0.0972
2000	155	-0.0065	0.3280	-9.02	-3.6914	-0.0374	0.0041	0.0547	1.0086	155	-0.0006	0.3575
2001	63	-0.0026	0.0824	1.37	-0.2598	-0.0427	-0.0080	0.0448	0.3841	63	-0.0033	0.0818
2002	38	-0.0126	0.0753	-1.67	-0.3165	-0.0396	-0.0067	0.0238	0.1210	38	-0.0139	0.0729
2003	51	-0.0040	0.0352	-0.24	-0.1034	-0.0262	-0.0005	0.0169	0.0804	51	-0.0074	0.0367
2004	60	-0.0003	0.0349	-1.22	-0.1349	-0.0148	0.0002	0.0234	0.0681	60	-0.0008	0.0293
2005	89	-0.0081	0.0433	-1.76	-0.2090	-0.0199	0.0004	0.0073	0.1301	89	-0.0081	0.0428
2006	129	-0.0024	0.0328	0.56	-0.1229	-0.0161	-0.0037	0.0083	0.1151	129	-0.0003	0.0319
2007	155	-0.0057	0.0370	-1.15	-0.2267	-0.0203	-0.0062	0.0102	0.1108	155	-0.0035	0.0297
2008	83	-0.0091	0.0792	-0.68	-0.2657	-0.0283	-0.0035	0.0270	0.2009	83	-0.0084	0.0688
2009	72	-0.0198	0.0738	-2.32	-0.4288	-0.0378	-0.0129	0.0126	0.1665	72	-0.0168	0.0672
2010	80	-0.0109	0.0694	-0.34	-0.2667	-0.0270	-0.0062	0.0185	0.2631	80	-0.0097	0.0668
2011	100	-0.0032	0.0595	-0.16	-0.2267	-0.0292	-0.0068	0.0242	0.2148	100	-0.0037	0.0547
2012	78	-0.0037	0.0379	-0.11	-0.1442	-0.0162	0.0003	0.0142	0.1394	78	-0.0009	0.0329
All	**1,683**	**0.0010**	**0.1223**	**-16.03**	**-3.6914**	**-0.0245**	**-0.0005**	**0.0278**	**1.0086**	**1,683**	**0.0023**	**0.1283**

Fig. 1: IV spreads

The chart plots the range of IV spreads (*t-1*) by year. Median values are represented by diamonds, the upper and lower quartiles by dots.

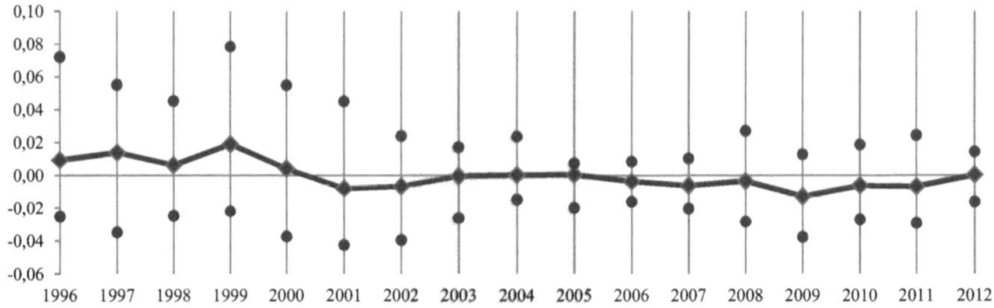

Table 2 reports summary statistics for *IV spread* and *IV spread*$_{ATM}$ on day *t–1*. Both measures have a (positive) mean close to zero and a standard deviation of 12 to 13%. The distribution seems to be highly negatively skewed. Interestingly, the means are positive for the years 1996 to 1999 but negative thereafter. The median IV spread is negative but also very close to zero. The minimum (–3.7) and the maximum (1.0) indicate that arbitrage opportunities might exist for some put-call pairs. In total, I have sufficient option data to calculate 1,683 spreads. Since *IV spread*$_{ATM}$ is not statistically different from *IV spread,* I report full summary statistics and regression tables for *IV spread* only. Figure 1 above plots the median IV spread as well as the upper and lower quartiles over time. It shows that the spread has decreased in magnitude since 1996 and that its range has narrowed. Since in theory the spread is zero, this observation could indicate that the markets have become more efficient, i.e. that there are fewer arbitrage opportunities in put and call options.

The second informed option trading proxy is the implied volatility skew. It is the difference between the implied volatility of an out-of-the-money put and the implied volatility of an at-the-money call option:

$$IVskew_{i.t} = IV_{i,t}^{OTMP} - IV_{i,t}^{ATMC} \tag{4}$$

Following Xing et al. (2010), I applied the following filters to construct this measure. ATM calls have a strike-to-stock price ratio between 95-105%; OTM puts between 80 and 95%. If more than one option with this feature is traded, the *IV* was calculated as an average over all traded options (weighted by open interest). This methodology differs from Xing et al. who weight by volume or use the option closest to 100% or 95% for ATM and OTM options, respectively. The weighting by open interest instead of volume makes this methodology consistent with the computation of IV spread. Additionally, the best offer price must be higher than $0.125 and the implied volatility needs to be between 3 and 200%.

Table 3 reports the IV skews for 994 pre-event days (*t–1*). On average, the IV skews are positive with a mean of 5.1% (median 4.5%) and a standard deviation of 8.6%. These numbers show that OTM puts are, as expected, relatively more expensive than ATM calls, suggesting that the average investor still buys OTM puts to insure herself against price drops and does not seem to have any information about the upcoming takeover bid one day before the announcement. The minimum reveals that some options do have a negative skew of up to –35.6%. This might be the result of option illiquidity and inherent market inefficiencies. It could also indicate excessive informed trading, i.e. rumors about the deal increase the demand for the ATM call options. The summary statistics again show a time effect: between 1996 and 2000, the yearly mean is about 1.9%. For the period between 2001 and 2012, in contrast, it is about 7.5%. A reason for the increase in IV skew might be the burst of the dotcom bubble in early 2000 and, subsequently, investors' "crashophobia", a concept typically used to explain the IV skew after the stock market crash in 1987. Figure 2 plots the quartiles of the IV skew distribution by year. The aggregate data does not show significant spikes around the financial crisis, something we would expect to observe in daily IV skew data. However, we do see the increase in IV skew over time and that the range between the upper and lower quartiles has narrowed in recent years.

TABLE 3: SUMMARY STATISTICS IV SKEW

This table summarizes the implied volatility skews (IV skew) for day *t-1*. IV skew is calculated as the difference between the implied volatility of an OTM put and the implied volatility of an ATM call option. OTM puts have a strike-to-stock price ratio of 80-95%, ATM calls of 95-105%. Implied volatilities of both puts and calls were weighted by open interest before calculating the skew. N is the number of events. MEAN represents the arithmetic average (equal-weighted) of all IV skew.

YEAR	N	MEAN	SD	SKEW	MIN	Q1	MEDIAN	Q3	MAX
1996	33	0.0139	0.0628	1.12	-0.1052	-0.0309	0.0044	0.0386	0.2310
1997	68	0.0147	0.0878	-0.54	-0.2166	-0.0255	0.0225	0.0817	0.1922
1998	103	0.0246	0.0994	-0.64	-0.3562	-0.0191	0.0220	0.0759	0.2652
1999	108	0.0137	0.0837	-0.29	-0.2631	-0.0343	0.0173	0.0661	0.2416
2000	93	0.0279	0.0999	0.07	-0.2868	-0.0167	0.0239	0.0712	0.3892
2001	35	0.0782	0.0936	1.25	-0.0558	0.0154	0.0489	0.1274	0.3463
2002	17	0.0739	0.0950	1.69	-0.0296	0.0356	0.0471	0.0918	0.3465
2003	30	0.0969	0.0887	1.09	-0.0269	0.0490	0.0777	0.1370	0.3238
2004	31	0.0666	0.0669	0.87	-0.0391	0.0180	0.0481	0.0916	0.2281
2005	43	0.0943	0.0934	0.96	-0.0777	0.0329	0.0588	0.1208	0.3252
2006	69	0.0615	0.0508	1.86	-0.0197	0.0303	0.0549	0.0822	0.2961
2007	91	0.0589	0.0715	1.41	-0.1083	0.0190	0.0429	0.0956	0.3862
2008	43	0.0792	0.0855	1.05	-0.0477	0.0345	0.0538	0.1055	0.3009
2009	42	0.0776	0.0632	1.60	-0.0130	0.0426	0.0622	0.0984	0.2833
2010	56	0.0747	0.0449	1.00	-0.0184	0.0461	0.0643	0.0999	0.2259
2011	77	0.0714	0.0641	1.22	-0.0247	0.0334	0.0573	0.0876	0.2513
2012	55	0.0721	0.0935	1.13	-0.1325	0.0176	0.0537	0.0890	0.3452
All	**994**	**0.0513**	**0.0855**	**0.22**	**-0.3562**	**0.0095**	**0.0449**	**0.0889**	**0.3892**

Fig. 2: IV skews

The chart plots the range of IV skews (*t-1*) by year. Median values are represented by diamonds, the upper and lower quartiles by dots.

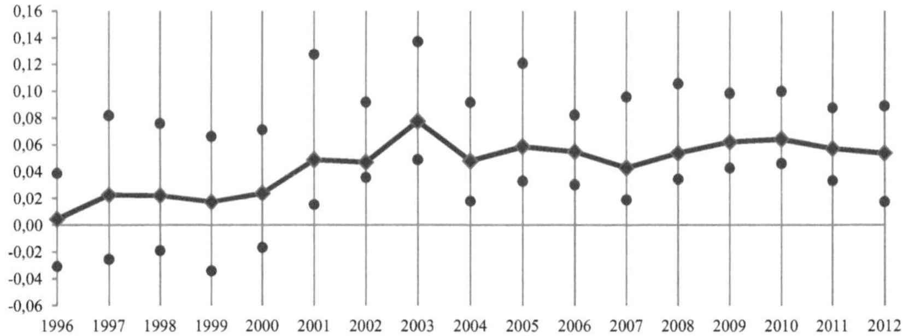

Finally, Roll et al (2010) define the third option trading proxy, O/S, as the ratio between the total option volume traded and the total stock volume traded for a given firm *i*:

$$O/S_{i,t} \ = \ (Vol_{i,t}^{option} \times 100)/Vol_{i,t}^{stock} \,, \qquad (5)$$

where *t* usually refers to a day. In this study, the O/S ratio one day before the takeover is very noisy and does not seem to have predictive power for announcement returns. Instead, I use the five-day average O/S ratio (*t–5* to *t–1*). The daily option volume is the aggregate of all option contracts traded on the underlying stock, multiplied by 100 (since each contract is for 100 shares). I report summary statistics for O/S in Table 4. The mean ratio is 7% with a standard deviation of 11%. The median is 3.5% and the distribution has a positive skew.

Because of the large difference between mean and median, I also calculated some in-between percentiles as well as the means of the trimmed (6.3%) and winsorized (5.2%) distribution using 5% and 95% as cut-offs (not tabulated). It seems that the results cannot be explained by the presence of outliers but by the fact that many options are not actively traded relative to their underlying stock. In fact, the first quartile is close to zero. This illiquidity might pose a problem during the later stages of this study. It also appears that the relative trading volume has decreased over time. This can be seen from Figure 3, which plots the O/S quartiles.

Due to the significant time-variation in all three variables, I will include time-fixed effects in my main regression models. The above statistics also suggest that illiquidity is a severe problem. Consequently, I will have a closer look at pre-announcement option liquidity and also include liquidity proxies in my regressions.

TABLE 4: SUMMARY STATISTICS O/S

This table summarizes the option-to-stock volume ratio (O/S) for days *t-5* to *t-1*. The ratio was calculated by dividing the total option volume over the five days preceding the announcement (multiplied by 100) by the total stock trading volume. N is the number of observations. MEAN represents the arithmetic average (equal-weighted) of all O/S. The minimum is not reported as it is zero in all years. 40%, 60%, and 95% represent percentiles.

YEAR	N	MEAN	SD	SKEW	Q1	40%	MEDIAN	60%	Q3	95%	Max
1996	106	7.12%	7.83%	2.47	2.08%	3.68%	4.39%	5.94%	9.63%	22.03%	50.31%
1997	139	11.07%	18.49%	7.22	2.28%	4.54%	6.39%	8.64%	15.68%	33.98%	194.41%
1998	210	7.82%	9.67%	2.24	1.08%	3.00%	4.46%	6.51%	10.86%	26.68%	58.34%
1999	227	7.11%	8.43%	2.34	1.87%	3.39%	4.24%	5.71%	9.27%	27.63%	48.23%
2000	180	6.95%	8.07%	2.39	1.69%	3.18%	4.07%	5.45%	9.47%	23.93%	54.81%
2001	83	4.28%	6.49%	2.70	0.47%	1.05%	1.59%	2.83%	4.66%	15.63%	34.10%
2002	52	2.23%	2.83%	2.52	0.36%	0.84%	1.28%	1.73%	3.09%	7.16%	15.59%
2003	60	6.87%	13.51%	4.65	0.83%	1.93%	3.59%	4.70%	6.77%	22.25%	90.72%
2004	78	5.26%	7.66%	2.17	0.48%	1.20%	2.01%	3.26%	5.79%	20.24%	36.48%
2005	106	6.00%	9.94%	3.42	0.63%	1.47%	2.35%	3.44%	6.88%	23.22%	65.58%
2006	149	7.30%	12.72%	4.46	0.56%	1.69%	2.98%	4.77%	10.00%	27.22%	107.26%
2007	184	7.88%	10.66%	2.34	0.64%	2.30%	3.99%	5.78%	10.92%	31.04%	65.63%
2008	109	6.39%	9.15%	2.04	0.44%	1.54%	2.41%	3.67%	7.27%	25.02%	42.34%
2009	92	5.71%	9.25%	3.75	0.28%	1.92%	3.10%	4.04%	7.22%	25.68%	64.02%
2010	107	7.75%	12.19%	2.00	0.30%	0.98%	2.26%	3.75%	10.46%	36.30%	51.29%
2011	139	7.90%	15.46%	3.93	0.22%	0.97%	1.74%	3.30%	8.14%	40.69%	118.05%
2012	125	5.57%	9.68%	2.75	0.09%	0.40%	1.32%	2.68%	6.51%	24.84%	50.05%
All	**2,146**	**7.04%**	**10.96%**	**5.00**	**0.72%**	**2.05%**	**3.47%**	**4.86%**	**8.88%**	**26.68%**	**194.41%**

Fig. 3: O/S ratios
The chart plots the range of O/S ratios (average over *t-5* to *t-1*) by year. Median values are represented by diamonds, the upper and lower quartiles by dots.

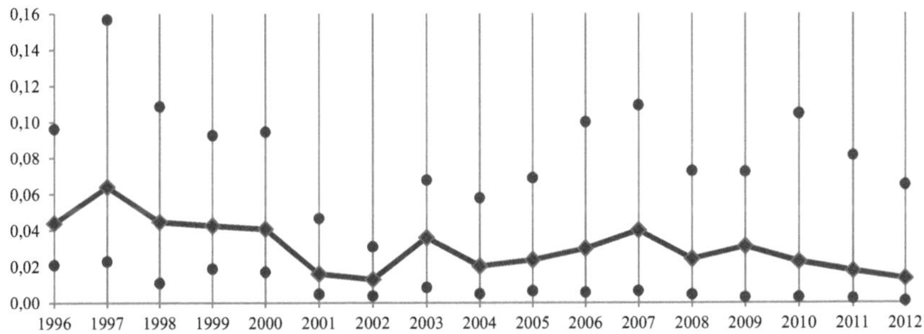

3.2.3 HYPOTHESIS TESTING

3.2.3.1 PRE-ANNOUNCEMENT LIQUIDITY

According to the first hypothesis, trading activity in options and stocks of target firms should rise to abnormal levels starting several days prior to the unscheduled takeover announcement due to the presence of informed traders. I adopt an approach by Amin and Lee (1997) who measure abnormal trading volume prior to earnings announcements by subtracting the mean daily volume on non-event days from the observed volume. The null hypothesis that trading volume is not abnormally high prior to a bid can be tested using a mean comparison t-test. Instead of volume, I use open interest and the bid-ask spread (difference between the best ask price and the best bid price scaled by the midpoint, cf. Driessen et al. 2012) to measure the liquidity of the options relative to non-event days. High open interest and a low bid-ask spread indicate higher liquidity. As for the benchmark, I calculate the mean open interest and bid-ask spread over a period of 50 trading days that ends on day *t–6*. This methodology should generally underestimate the abnormal liquidity of the options before the bid because the benchmark period can also include other news events (e.g. earnings), which should increase the average liquidity. In an alternative setting, the benchmark is therefore adjusted by excluding all days surrounding quarterly/annual earnings announcements (*t–5* to *t+5*). To capture the untainted effect of informed option trading, I only include the first reported announcement event for each firm.

Elevated option liquidity prior to a takeover bid would indicate that traders utilize their private information to also trade in options of target firms. In a second step, I test whether liquidity measures can indeed anticipate the arrival of a takeover bid by running a logit regression on a panel of daily option data. The dependent variable takes the value of 1 if a takeover bid arrives over the course of the next 3 days, and 0 otherwise. The independent variable is the daily liquidity of the option, measured in open interest. Alternatively, liquidity is proxied by the average bid-ask spread. Compared to OLS, a logit model has the advantage that the modeled "probability" of a takeover bid can never be negative or larger than 1. On the downside, the economic interpretation of the coefficients is more difficult because the model is non-linear. To overcome this difficulty, I also report odds ratios. The significance of the coefficients can be determined using a standard t-test. The estimation model has the form:

$$\begin{aligned} P_{i,t} \ = \ & \beta_1 + \beta_2 LIQ_{i,t} + \beta_3 margin_{i,t} + \beta_4 ROE_{i,t} + \beta_5 size_{i,t} + \ \beta_6 block_{i,t} \\ & + \beta_7 industry_{i,t} + \varepsilon_{i,t} \ , \end{aligned} \qquad (6)$$

where P_i is the probability that there will be a takeover announcement within three days. LIQ is either the open interest (in 1,000 contracts) or the bid-ask spread, as defined above. To avoid an overestimation of the liquidity coefficient, the specification should also control for other variables that might influence the probability of a takeover bid. My model therefore includes two profitability proxies (profit margin defined as net income divided by revenue, and return on equity), firm size (the base-2 logarithm of the total asset value), the percentage of shares held by all blockholders (those with a stake higher than 5%), and the target industry (2-digit SIC code). All control variables reflect quarterly information. They were matched with the daily option data by backdating both the option date and the financial statement report date to the first month of the respective quarter, i.e. January, April, July, and October.

3.2.3.2 Cross-sectional regression and control variables

The main research question and hypothesis revolve around the effect of target and deal characteristics on the predictive power of option trading proxies for announcement returns of target firms (i.e. takeover premiums). To test the hypothesis that these characteristics have any effect at all, I first need to replicate the results found in the literature, particularly in Chan et al. (2012). That is, I test whether pre-announcement IV spread, IV skew, and O/S can predict the stock price reaction of target firms upon the announcement of a takeover bid. Chan et al. discuss target returns very briefly but mainly focus on acquirers. They also do not test the O/S ratio in the context of target firms.

In my analysis, I regress CARs on the three option trading proxies. Due to the correlation between the main predictor variables, I run separate regressions for each one of them, introducing an omitted variable bias. Appendix 2 shows the correlation matrix of the three proxies. Following Chan et al. (2012), I include a number of control variables: pre-month buy-and-hold stock return (*return*),[2] if SDC classifies the takeover as *completed*, *hostile*, a *tender* offer or if it began as a *rumor* (all binary dummy variables); a dummy for deals financed with more than 50% cash (*cash*), firm *size* (measured by the natural logarithm of market equity), and the natural logarithm of the book-to-market ratio (*BM*). I also add year-fixed and industry-fixed effects due to the apparent time variation (and expected variation across industries) within the three informed option trading proxies. As motivated in section 3.2.1, I include a control for stock return skewness (*returnSkew*), which is measured over the 30 days preceding the takeover. Following Driessen et al. (2012), I also control for pre-announcement 30-day stock return volatility (*returnSD*). The control *acqIndustry* is a dummy variable that equals 1 if the target and the acquirer share the same 2-digit SIC code. I add this control because it could be that acquirers from the same industry pay more for a target than firms that only want to diversify their portfolios. *acqType* equals 1 if the acquirer is a publicly listed company, and zero otherwise. This dummy is included because Bargeron et al. (2008) find that public acquirers pay higher premiums than private bidders. Finally, I control for a number of option and stock liquidity measures. *optBidAsk* is the equal-weighted, five-day average option bid-ask spread. Each option's bid-ask spread is scaled by its respective midpoint, and for each day these spreads are summed and weighted by open interest. *optOI* is the equal-weighted, five-day average open interest. *abnSVol* is a control for abnormal stock

[2] I calculate this return over a period of 30 trading days, ending on day *t–1*.

trading. It is calculated by dividing the stock volume on day *t–1* by the prior 30-day average trading volume. *abnOVol* is the corresponding measure for abnormal option volume. If my main option trading proxies do have predictive power for announcement day returns, this predictability might be augmented by this abnormal trading activity. The resulting regression equation is as follows:

$$\begin{aligned} CAR_i = {} & \beta_0 + \beta_{1,i} PROXY_{i,t-1} \\ & + \beta_{2,i} return_{i,[t-30,t-1]} + \beta_{2,i} returnSD_{i,[t-30,t-1]} + \beta_{3,i} returnSkew_{i,[t-30,t-1]} \\ & + \beta_{4,i} completed_i + \beta_{5,i} hostile_i + \beta_{6,i} tender_i + \beta_{7,i} rumor_i + \beta_{8,i} cash_i \\ & + \beta_{9,i} acqIndustry_i + \beta_{10,i} size_i + \beta_{11,i} BM_i + \beta_{12,i} acqType_i \\ & + \beta_{13,i} optBidAsk_{i,[t-5,t-1]} + \beta_{14,i} optOI_{i,[t-5,t-1]} + \beta_{15,i} abnSVol_{i,t-1} \\ & + \beta_{16,i} abnOVol_{i,t-1} + \varepsilon_i \ , \end{aligned} \tag{7}$$

where *PROXY* takes the value of either pre-announcement *IV spread*, *IV skew*, or *O/S*, as defined above. The regression model is executed stepwise to assess the incremental effect of the controls. Since the residual plots in the main regressions suggest the presence of heteroskedasticity, I report all results with t-statistics based on White's (1980) robust standard errors. I refrain from clustering standard errors (by firm) because there would not be sufficient within-cluster variation (only a limited number of firms had more than one takeover attempt). Also, multicollinearity is tested by means of correlation analysis and by estimating the variance inflation factors (VIF) for each coefficient. While some variables are moderately correlated, VIFs remain small, suggesting that multicollinearity is not an issue.

3.2.3.3 Effect of deal characteristics on CAR predictability

Finally, I test the effects of other deal and target characteristics on the predictive power of the three option proxies. Considering the arguments leading to hypothesis *H3*, this predictability might be higher for deals financed primarily with cash as opposed to deals financed with stock. The regression model I use to test this hypothesis has a two-way factorial design, which means that it includes the two main effects (the continuous variable PROXY and a binary dummy) as well as an interaction term, allowing me to assess the impact of the amount of cash used on the relation between the respective informed option proxy and the CAR. Put differently, the interaction term does not only change the intercept of the regression line for a certain reference group (which is what a regular dummy does) but changes the slope of the regression line as well.

$$CAR_i = \beta_0 + \beta_{1,i}PROXY_{i,t-1} + \beta_{2,i}financing_i + \beta_{3,i}(financing_i \times PROXY_{i,t-1}) \quad (8)$$
$$+\beta_{4,i}controls_{i,t-1} + \varepsilon_i$$

The dummy variable *financing* takes the value 1 if the deal was financed with less than 25% cash and 0 if cash amounted to more than 75% of total financing. Previous research shows that the market reaction to mixed financing (e.g. 25-75% cash) is difficult to evaluate. Excluding this range allows me to directly compare low-cash and high-cash transactions, but it reduces the sample by 285 takeovers. The mean percentage of cash used in the low-cash group is 0.86%, whereas it is 98.4% in the high-cash group. If the mode of payment is relevant for the predictive power of the option proxies, the coefficient of the interaction term should be significantly different from zero.

In order to test hypothesis H4, I follow Berger et al. (1997) and define the percentage of total shares held by top-management and board composition as proxies for managerial entrenchment. A higher ownership stake in the firm should increase managerial entrenchment. Board composition is the percentage of outside/independent directors on the board. The higher this fraction, the lower the expected degree of managerial entrenchment. The regression model looks as follows:

$$CAR_i = \beta_0 + \beta_{1,i}PROXY_{i,t-1} + \beta_{2,i}entrench_{i,t-1} + \beta_{3,i}(entrench_{i,t-1} \times PROXY_{i,t-1}) \quad (9)$$
$$+\beta_{4,i}controls_{i,t-1} + \varepsilon_i \ ,$$

where *entrench* represents either the *ExecutiveShares* or the *Board* dummy variable. *ExecutiveShares* is equal to 1 if the officers and directors own a combined stake of more than 10% in the firm, and given a value of 0 otherwise. *Board* equals 1 if the percentage of outsiders on the board exceeds 75%, and 0 otherwise. Both dummies are lagged by one year to ensure that the data is from before the takeover announcement (WRDS' Corporate Library does not mention the reporting date of the proxy information). Again, we need to reject hypothesis H4 if the coefficient of the interaction term (β_3) is insignificant.

Finally, I test hypothesis H5 by interacting the three informed option trading proxies with an industry dummy (*acqIndustry*) that equals 1 if both the acquirer and the target share the same two-digit SIC code, and given a value of 0 otherwise. The model looks as follows:

$$CAR_i = \beta_0 + \beta_{1,i}PROXY_{i,t-1} + \beta_{2,i}acqIndustry_i + \beta_{3,i}(acqIndustry_i \times PROXY_{i,t-1}) \quad (10)$$
$$+\beta_{4,i}controls_{i,t-1} + \varepsilon_i \ .$$

If some traders have special inside information regarding a certain industry, β_3 should be significant. The next section summarizes the empirical results of my analyses.

4. Empirical results

4.1 Option liquidity

In hypothesis H1, I argue that the liquidity of target options increases before (unscheduled) takeover announcements due to the presence of informed traders. Testing this hypothesis lays the foundations for the remaining hypothesis tests. The expectation is to find higher liquidity, i.e. positive abnormal open interest and negative abnormal bid-ask spreads. Table 5 shows the results of one-sample mean comparison tests for both measures over the five days prior to a takeover bid and on the announcement day itself.

TABLE 5: OPTION LIQUIDITY

This table shows the abnormal open interest ("OI", Panel A) and bid-ask spread ("BA", Panel B) for the five days before the takeover announcement. OI is the sum of open interest over all options traded during a day. BA is defined as the difference between the best ask price and the best bid price, scaled by the midpoint. The daily BA is the average BA over all traded options. Abnormal open interest/bid-ask spread was calculated by subtracting the mean daily OI/BA over a 50-day benchmark period [*t-55, t-6*] from the observed OI/BA on each day. For firms with more than one takeover announcement, only the first one was included. Days are reported relative to the announcement day t. SD is the standard deviation. t-statistics are in parentheses. *, **, *** denote statistical significance at the 10%, 5%, and 1% level, respectively.

Panel A: Abnormal open interest

Day	t-5	t-4	t-3	t-2	t-1	t
Abn. Open Interest	517.72	637.24	754.99	814.29	944.19	810.16
SD (in 1,000)	20.61	20.04	20.33	21.14	22.37	21.29
t-stat	(1.11)	(1.41)	(1.64)	(1.70)*	(1.87)*	(1.68)*

Panel B: Abnormal Bid-Ask Spread

Day	t-5	t-4	t-3	t-2	t-1	t
Abn. Bid-Ask Spread	-0.007	-0.009	-0.010	-0.011	-0.017	-0.058
SD	0.154	0.152	0.156	0.161	0.166	0.194
t-stat	(-2.06)**	(-2.56)***	(-2.89)***	(-3.10)***	(-4.51)***	(-13.11)***

Both liquidity proxies have the expected sign and are statistically significant. The abnormal open interest ("OI") rises monotonically from 517 on day *t–5* to 944 on day *t–1* and levels off on the event day. The results are significant at the 10% level on the two days preceding the bid, suggesting that informed traders do demand more options on these days. The economic significance is of course questionable. Considering that even small target firms have several hundred thousand or even millions of stocks, an increase by a few hundred options in OI does not seem to be much. However, the mean daily OI during the 50-day benchmark period is about 8,850. The abnormal OI on day *t–1* therefore corresponds to an increase by 11%. This is similar to what Amin and Lee (1997) find for abnormal option trading volume before earnings announcements. On the other hand, the standard deviation is exceeding 20,000, which shows that some firms not only actively trade a greater volume of options but also have substantial (negative) abnormal liquidity before the announcement. Panel B shows the results for the abnormal bid-ask spread ("BA"). This proxy is negative and highly significant on all five days before the bid, ranging from –0.007 on *t–5* to –0.017 on *t–1*. This corresponds to a drop of up to 5.6% compared to the mean benchmark spread of 0.303. These results confirm that target firms experience some informed, pre-announcement option trading. I can therefore reject the null hypothesis of H1 that abnormal liquidity is zero. In Appendix 3, I repeat this analysis but exclude days surrounding earnings announcements from the benchmark. The abnormal bid-ask spread is less significant on days *t–5* and *t–4*, but the overall results seem to be robust.

In a second step, I use a logit regression to test whether OI and BA have predictive power for takeover announcements, i.e. if they affect the probability that an announcement occurs within the next three days. Panel A of Table 6 summarizes the regression results for a pooled logit model with time-fixed effects. Open interest by itself is statistically highly significant, but only very small economically. An increase of OI by 1,000 contracts increases the likelihood of a takeover bid by only 0.1%. Considering that the mean daily OI over all pre-announcement days is about 8,400, this is really a marginal effect. The bid-ask spread is not significant by itself, but only after including the controls for firm profitability (model 5). The coefficient of –0.11 (or –0.33 in model 5) means that the odds of a takeover bid decrease by (1 / exp(–0.11) – 1 =) 11.6% to 39% if the BA increases by 1. This effect is still small considering that mean daily BA has a standard deviation of only 0.19, but it is certainly not as marginal an effect as we have seen in the case of open interest.

As control variables I include two proxies for firm profitability because I expect that more profitable firms are more likely to become targets. In some cases, e.g. private equity buyouts, a firm might also become a target if performance has been poor. But in general, profitable firms should be more attractive for acquirers. I find that profit margin has a positive effect on takeover probability (low significance). This is consistent with my expectations that more profitable firms are more likely to become targets. On the other hand, return on equity is negatively related to the probability of a bid. This changes only when firm size is included in the regression (see model 3 and 6). Size (measured in total asset value) should be positively related to the takeover probability because larger firms have more analyst coverage and might also be less risky. In fact, the highly significant odds ratios suggest that doubling[3] the firm size will increase the odds of a takeover bid by 6.9 to 7.5%. Also consistent with expectations, the presence of blockholders decreases the probability of a takeover. This control only becomes slightly significant after controlling for year-fixed effects. The target's industry

[3] Asset value was transformed to a base 2 logarithm for ease of interpretation.

seems to have no impact. Without clustering standard errors by firm, the profitability and size coefficients become significant at the 1% level. This is because within each cluster/firm, the independent variables are obtained quarterly and therefore highly persistent. Clustering removes the downward bias in the standard errors.

TABLE 6: PROBABILITY OF TAKEOVER ANNOUNCEMENT

This table shows logit regression estimates of the probability that a takeover announcement occurs within the next three days. Panel A summarizes the results of a pooled logit regression with clustered standard errors (by firm). Panel B reports estimates of the fixed-effects model (also by firm) which omits the industry variable from Panel A because industry remains constant for each firm. The regressions include all days prior to each firm's first announcement day. Open interest (in 1,000) and bid-ask spread represent mean daily values. In contrast to Table 5, the liquidity measures are not measured in abnormal terms. Margin is the firms profit margin, i.e. net income divided by total revenue, ROE is return on equity, size is the logarithm (base 2) of total assets, block is the percentage of shares held by blockholders (>5%), and industry is the 2-digit SIC code. Two-tailed p-values are in parentheses. The statistic below the p-value is the odds ratio. *, **, *** denote statistical significance at the 10%, 5%, and 1% level, respectively. In Panel A, § denotes statistical significance at the 1% level if standard errors are not clustered by firm.

Panel A: Pooled logit model

	(1)	(2)	(3)	(4)	(5)	(6)
Open Interest (in 1,000)	0.001	0.003	0.001			
	(0.009)***§	(0.001)***§	(0.606)			
	1.001	1.003	1.001			
Bid-Ask spread				-0.110	-0.329	0.027
				(0.286)	(0.019)**§	(0.896)
				0.896	0.720	1.027
Margin		0.022	0.030		0.022	0.029
		(0.067)*§	(0.084)*§		(0.068)*§	(0.075)*§
		1.022	1.030		1.022	1.029
ROE		-0.001	0.070		-0.001	0.071
		(0.565)§	(0.202)§		(0.512)§	(0.235)§
		0.999	1.072		0.999	1.073
Size			0.067			0.078
			(0.000)***§			(0.000)***§
			1.069			1.075
Block			-0.410			-0.417
			(0.070)*			(0.065)*
			0.664			0.659
Industry			0.000			0.000
			(0.950)			(0.980)
			1.000			1.000
Year fixed effects		YES	YES		YES	YES
Intercept	-3.893	-4.110	-5.047	-3.850	-4.015	-5.105
	(0.000)***§	(0.000)***§	(0.000)***§	(0.000)***§	(0.000)***§	(0.000)***§
N	291,717	244,442	89,250	291,717	244,442	89,250
Pseudo R-square	0.0002	0.0033	0.0074	0	0.0028	0.0044

In Panel B, I repeat my analysis in a panel framework with fixed-effects (FE) in order to control for omitted variables, which seem to be a problem in the pooled regression as the pseudo R-square is close to zero in all specifications. While FE discard all of the variation between individual firms (e.g. industry), it allows for the capture of the unbiased effects of all predictors within each firm. The results show that both OI and BA are statistically significant on their own and after including the controls (except for BA in model 6). They also tend to have larger coefficients. Nevertheless, the effect is still marginal for open interest. For the bid-ask spread, an increase by 1 unit decreases the odds of a takeover bid by about 75%.

This significant effect vanishes after controlling for firm size. In the fixed-effects framework, profitability loses its significance. Further, the odds of a takeover increase 120-fold if firm size is doubled! This noteworthy finding might be due to some multicollinearity issues since the asset value is correlated with OI (41%) and BA (25%). If firm size is the only predictor variable in the regression, its coefficient decreases to 2.2 (or an odds ratio of 8.8), which is still remarkable. In summary, we see that liquidity does increase before a takeover announcement, possibly because of the presence of informed traders. Both abnormal open interest and the bid-ask spread have the expected sign. Finally, both liquidity proxies have some predictive power for the arrival of takeover bids. However, this effect is marginal and dominated by firm size; and the low pseudo-R-square in the pooled model suggests that the results are very weak and should be handled with high caution.

TABLE 6: PROBABILITY OF TAKEOVER ANNOUNCEMENT (CONTINUED)

	Panel B: Fixed-effects logit model					
	(1)	(2)	(3)	(4)	(5)	(6)
Open Interest	0.008	0.007	0.003			
(in 1,000)	(0.000)***	(0.000)***	(0.000)***			
	1.008	1.007	1.000			
Bid-Ask spread				-0.551	-0.566	0.021
				(0.000)***	(0.000)***	(0.920)
				0.576	0.568	1.001
Margin		0.005	0.032		0.005	0.034
		(0.224)	(0.426)		(0.272)	(0.393)
		1.005	1.032		1.005	1.034
ROE		-0.003	0.018		-0.003	0.025
		(0.189)	(0.750)		(0.241)	(0.659)
		0.997	1.018		0.997	1.026
Size			4.786			4.823
			(0.000)***			(0.000)***
			119.772			124.354
Block			1.026			1.033
			(0.299)			(0.296)
			2.790			2.809
N	291,709	191,662	64,441	291,709	191,662	64,441
Firms	1,961	1,294	424	1,961	1,294	424
LR Chi2	99	74.77	137.78	32.97	29.44	125.86

4.2 Predictive power of options for CARs

4.2.1 Sorted portfolio approach

Before running a more formal regression analysis, I test the predictability of IV spread, IV skew, and O/S using a sorted portfolio approach. This approach is appealing due to its simplicity and because it reduces firm-level noise in the data. On the other hand, only one or two variables can be tested in this framework without reducing the size of the sub-portfolios too much. Sorting portfolios only serves as a preliminary test. The main hypothesis tests (the effect of certain deal and target characteristics on the predictive power of the three informed option trading proxies) will be performed by means of regressions in section 4.2.3.

I construct quintile portfolios based on IV spread and IV skew on day *t–1*. Adding to the previous literature, I also build quintiles on the five-day average O/S ratio between *t–5* and *t–1*. For each portfolio of firms, I report the average Carhart CAR over the two-day event window. The CAR of the high-minus-low portfolio is the abnormal return an investor could (theoretically) earn if she went long in the high portfolio and short in the low portfolio on day *t–1*. Of course, the expected returns of simply going long in all stocks of target firms would be a lot higher, provided the investor is indeed informed about all announcements. It is thus more practical to see the high-low return as a gauge of the economic significance of the respective option variable. I expect the target CAR to increase with IV spread and decrease with IV skew because of demand pressures (calls become more expensive). The same reasoning should result in a positive relationship between O/S and CAR. If informed traders expect the takeover announcement, demand for options in general and for calls in particular should increase. More importantly, because of the leverage in options, option demand should increase more than stock demand.

The results in Panel B of Table 7 support the story behind IV skew: the low-skew portfolio has a mean CAR of 15% and the high-skew portfolio's CAR is 12.4%. However, while Chan et al. (2012) find a highly significant negative relation for both acquiring firms (high-low –1.37%) and target firms (–5.09%), my results indicate no significant difference between the two (t-stat of –1.54). Also, the relationship is far from being monotonic. For IV spread, Cremers and Weinbaum (2010) find a significantly positive 2-week hedge portfolio mean return of 20bps; and Chan et al. (2012) show that the high-low CAR for their sample of acquirers (targets) is 0.9% (2.7%). My results do not support these findings, even though my sample does not significantly differ from that of Chan et al. The high-low CAR is slightly negative (–0.1%) and not significant (see Panel A). Only if I limit my sample to firms with a market capitalization of more than $500 million, the difference is positive (1.7%), but still insignificant. All results for this larger-firm sample are tabulated in Appendix 4. Finally, the results for O/S (Panel C) seem to be in contradiction with the economic intuition that informed traders will prefer options over stocks due to the options' leverage. The relationship between O/S and CAR is almost monotonically negative with a high-low difference of –6.5%, which is significant at the 99% confidence level. This result is robust to using absolute CARs (originally proposed by Roll et al. (2010) for earnings announcements) and to the exclusion of small firms (<$500 in equity, see Appendix 4). It might be that traders that have (or believe to have) private information about the takeover perceive the purchase of stocks as more attractive than that of call options, perhaps because of the lower option liquidity in target firms. Lower liquidity will increase both the direct (commissions) and indirect (spread) costs of purchasing and of closing out the call. Since a call is expected to be deep in the money after the takeover announcement, the liquidity problem might even be more severe than before. In the case of target firms, stocks might therefore be the less expensive and less risky choice for informed traders. However, it still seems puzzling that the lack of liquidity could outweigh the advantages of leverage.

With regard to hypothesis H2 – that informed option trading proxies predict target announcement returns – portfolio sorting yields mixed results. I can reject hypothesis H2 for IV spread, but there is some evidence that IV skew might be a viable predictor for CARs. H2 cannot be rejected for O/S as this proxy seems to be a strongly negatively related to CARs.

TABLE 7: QUINTILE PORTFOLIO SORTING

Panels A, B, C of this table shows the average target CARs of quintile portfolios formed on IV spread, IV skew and O/S, respectively. The CARs are computed for an event window from *t* to *t+1* with an estimation period of *t-205* to *t-6*, using a 4-factor model. The three informed options trading proxies are defined as in Tables 2 to 4. The last column represents the difference between the High-quintile and the Low-quintile portfolio. t-statistics are in parentheses. *, **, *** denote statistical significance at the 10%, 5%, and 1% level, respectively.

Panel A: IV Spread (t-1)

	Low	2	3	4	High	High-Low
Mean CAR	16.42%	16.12%	15.45%	15.58%	16.29%	-0.13%
SD CAR	21.14%	17.14%	15.60%	18.45%	23.22%	-
t-stat	(14.26)***	(17.26)***	(18.16)***	(15.5)***	(12.86)***	(-0.07)

Panel B: IV Skew (t-1)

	Low	2	3	4	High	High-Low
Mean CAR	15.01%	15.07%	16.08%	14.48%	12.40%	-2.61%
SD CAR	18.66%	18.07%	18.11%	16.32%	15.02%	-
t-stat	(11.35)***	(11.77)***	(12.53)***	(12.52)***	(11.61)***	(-1.54)

Panel C: O/S ratio (average t-5 to t-1)

	Low	2	3	4	High	High-Low
Mean CAR	19.23%	17.80%	18.01%	15.90%	12.77%	-6.46%
SD CAR	23.39%	21.44%	23.46%	18.96%	18.80%	-
t-stat	(17.05)***	(17.19)***	(15.90)***	(17.37)***	(14.07)***	(-4.46)***

4.2.2 Regression results

This section replicates the regression analysis in Chan et al. (2012) for target firms. Specifically, target announcement CARs are regressed on IV spread, IV skew, and O/S. As discussed before, I expect to find a positive relation between IV spread and CAR and a negative relation between IV skew and CAR. In the existing literature, a positive relation is found between O/S and absolute announcement CARs in the context of earnings surprises and takeover announcements by bidding firms. In my analysis, I do not use absolute CARs because target announcement CARs are expected to be positive on average, i.e. informed trading should be associated with higher demand for calls. Tables 8 to 10 show the regression results for target firms. As the residual plots suggest the presence of heteroskedasticity, the test statistics are calculated using White's (1980) robust standard errors.

Table 8 presents the results for IV spread. In contrast to Cremers and Weinbaum (2010), Driessen et al. (2012), and Chan et al. (2012), I find no evidence that pre-announcement IV spread is (positively) related to announcement CARs of target firms, i.e. call options do not seem to be subject to higher demand pressure than put options. The coefficient of IV spread is insignificant by itself and in all other model specifications. Depending on the model, it ranges from –1% to 2%. Due to the expected noise in the one-day lagged IV spread, I repeat all regressions with the three-day equal-weighted average IV spread (from day *t–3* to *t–1*). Here, the coefficient increases to 4-8% but is still insignificant (see Appendix 5 for the results). The positive coefficient conforms to economic intuition that call options should be relatively more expensive than put options if good news is expected. There are two possible explanations for the insignificance of the results. Firstly, option liquidity could generally be too low and daily implied volatilities too noisy to begin with. In fact, there seems to be a high variation in the average implied volatilities of individual options even over short periods of time. Second, the relative option illiquidity could prompt informed traders to trade in the stock market instead. The liquidity tests in section 4.1 suggest that option liquidity does rise before the announcement. However, demand for stocks might be subject to an even larger increase. The O/S ratio will hopefully shed some light on this question.

TABLE 8: CROSS-SECTIONAL REGRESSIONS OF TARGET CAR ON IV SPREAD

This table presents cross-sectional regression results of target announcement returns on IV spread and a number of control variables. The CARs are computed for an event window from *t* to *t+1* with an estimation period of *t-205* to *t-6*, using a 4-factor model. IV spread for day *t-1* is calculated according to Cremers and Weinbaum (2010). Return is the buy-and-hold return for the target stock between *t-30* and *t-1*. ReturnSD and returnSkew are the standard deviation and skewness of returns (same period). Completed, hostile, tender, rumor, cash50 ,and acqIndustry are dummy variables that take the value of 1 if the bid was ultimately successful, a tender offer, was preceded by a rumor, was financed with more than 50% cash, or if the target and the acquirer share the same 2-digit SIC code, respectively. Size is the ln of the target's equity value at announcement, BM represents the book-to-market ratio, and acqType is a dummy that equals 1 if the bidder is a publicly listed firm as opposed to a private firm. The remaining controls are liquidity proxies: optBidAsk and optOI are the average bid-ask spread and open interest from *t-5* to *t-1*. AbnSVol and abnOVol are the abnormal stock and option trading volumes on *t-1*, with normal trading volume being estimated over days *t-30* to *t-1*. t-statistics (in parentheses) are reported using White's (1980) heteroskedasticity robust standard errors. *, **, *** denote statistical significance at the 10%, 5%, and 1% level, respectively.

	Dependent Variable: $CAR_{i, [0,1]}$						
	(1)	(2)	(3)	(4)	(5)	(6)	(7)
IV spread (t-1)	0.02	0.01	-0.01	-0.01	0.01	0.00	0.00
	(0.49)	(0.25)	(-0.29)	(-0.33)	(0.21)	(-0.11)	(0.02)
Return		-0.06	-0.14	-0.15	-0.14	-0.14	-0.15
		(-1.78)*	(-4.09)***	(-4.4)***	(-3.9)***	(-3.84)***	(-4.04)***
ReturnSD		0.10	0.32	0.00	0.01	0.26	0.09
		(0.29)	(0.84)	(0.01)	(0.03)	(0.59)	(0.19)
ReturnSkew		-0.01	-0.01	0.00	0.00	0.00	0.00
		(-2.14)***	(-1.36)	(-0.53)	(-0.76)	(-0.29)	(0.17)
Completed			0.04	0.05	0.02	0.02	0.03
			(3.38)***	(3.75)***	(1.52)	(1.5)	(1.90)*
Hostile			0.05	0.04	0.03	0.02	0.03
			(2.02)**	(1.48)	(1.08)	(0.71)	(0.90)
Tender			0.09	0.07	0.08	0.09	0.08
			(5.8)***	(4.58)***	(4.58)***	(4.92)***	(4.74)***
Rumor			-0.09	-0.11	-0.08	-0.07	-0.08
			(-7.17)***	(-7.42)***	(-5.15)***	(-4.19)***	(-4.55)***
Cash50			0.09	0.08	0.09	0.09	0.08
			(8.5)***	(6.62)***	(6.94)***	(6.5)***	(5.95)***
AcqIndustry			0.02	0.03	0.01	0.01	0.01
			(2.45)**	(2.76)***	(0.90)	(0.80)	(1.20)
Size					0.00	0.00	0.00
					(-0.57)	(0.73)	(0.34)
BM					-0.02	-0.02	-0.03
					(-2.32)**	(-2.58)***	(-3.04)***
AcqType					0.07	0.08	0.07
					(4.79)***	(5.18)***	(4.54)***
OptBidAsk						0.15	0.11
						(3.31)***	(2.24)**
OptOI						0.00	0.00
						(-0.79)	(-0.99)
AbnSVol						-0.02	-0.01
						(-2.98)***	(-2.73)***
AbnOVol						0.00	0.00
						(0.62)	(0.47)
Industry fixed effects				YES	YES	YES	YES
Year fixed effects				YES			YES
Intercept	0.16	0.17	0.08	-0.01	-0.18	-0.24	-0.21
	(33.99)***	(17.49)***	(4.78)***	(-0.21)	(-2.14)**	(-3.11)***	(-2.48)**
N	1683	1683	1447	1447.00	1239	1230	1230
R-square	0.0001	0.0114	0.1793	0.2519	0.2451	0.2656	0.2894
Adj. R-square	-0.0005	0.0091	0.1735	0.2034	0.1964	0.2151	0.2298

Most of the control coefficients have the expected sign. Ceteris paribus, a one standard deviation increase in stock price run-up (*return*) or *t–1* abnormal stock trading volume (*abnSVol*) would reduce the announcement CAR by 3.4% or 2.2%, respectively. Pre-announcement rumors have a similarly strong effect: deals that are preceded by rumors have more than 8% lower CARs on average than non-rumored deals. Consistent with the existing literature, bids that are ultimately successful have a 2–5% higher CAR than failed ones, though the coefficient is not significant in all specifications. It thus seems that the market correctly anticipates the outcome of the deal. Tender offers have about 9% higher CARs than other types of deals. Moeller et al. (2004) ascribe this to the notion that most tender offers are cash-financed acquisitions by public firms. My data confirms that the cash and tender dummies are correlated. Consistent with the pecking order theory by Myers and Majluf (1984), cash deals (deals financed with more than 50% cash) have a 9% higher CAR than stock deals. As suggested by Bargeron et al. (2008), deals initiated by public bidders have 7-8% higher CARs compared to takeovers by private bidders. Also the results partially confirm my hypothesis that CARs are higher if the bidder and the target are from the same industry, i.e. bidders pay a 1–3% premium if the target complements their core business (*acqIndustry* is only significant in models 3 and 4). Note that the inclusion of the aforementioned dummy variables significantly raises the R-square of the model. Finally, the option bid-ask spread positively predicts CARs: a one standard deviation increase in the spread raises CAR by about 1.4%. This result seems counterintuitive because higher option liquidity (i.e. lower bid-ask spread) is associated with the presence of informed traders, which in turn should be positively related to CARs. On the other hand, this could simply be a spurious relationship. After all, the second liquidity proxy, open interest, as well as abnormal option trading volume are not significant.

Table 9 shows the regression results for IV skew. Consistent with Xing et al. (2010) and Chan et al. (2012), IV skew is negatively related to CAR with a coefficient of –0.08 to –0.16. The coefficients remain insignificant unless year dummies are added (e.g. model 2). The respective coefficient of –0.16 suggests that a one standard deviation increase in IV skew leads to a 0.08 standard deviation (1.4%) decrease in predicted CAR. Informed option trading therefore seems to flatten the implied volatility smirk by applying buying pressure on ATM calls and selling pressure on OTM puts. Controlling for year-fixed effects is necessary because, as we have seen in the summary statistics of IV skew, the mean IV skew varies greatly over time (particularly from before to after 2001). Interestingly, Chan et al. (2012) find a significant relationship for a smaller sample of target firms even without controlling for time.

TABLE 9: CROSS-SECTIONAL REGRESSIONS OF TARGET CAR ON IV SKEW

This table presents cross-sectional regression results of target announcement returns on IV skew and a number of control variables. The CARs are computed for an event window from *t* to *t+1* with an estimation period of *t-205* to *t-6*, using a 4-factor model. IV skew for day *t-1* is calculated according to Xing et al. (2010). All control variables are defined as in Table 8. t-statistics (in parentheses) are reported using White's (1980) heteroskedasticity robust standard errors. *, **, *** denote statistical significance at the 10%, 5%, and 1% level, respectively.

	Dependent Variable: $CAR_{i,[0,1]}$							
	(1)	(2)	(3)	(4)	(5)	(6)	(7)	(8)
IV skew (t-1)	-0.10	-0.16	-0.08	-0.09	-0.14	-0.10	-0.12	-0.14
	-1.55	(-2.29)**	(-1.2)	(-1.3)	(-1.92)*	(-1.47)	(-1.59)	(-1.77)*
Return			-0.07	-0.19	-0.18	-0.17	-0.16	-0.16
			(-2.16)**	(-5.75)***	(-5.07)***	(-4.65)***	(-4.51)***	(-4.36)***
ReturnSD			0.30	0.77	0.44	0.15	0.24	0.33
			(0.96)	(2.64)***	(1.36)	(0.42)	(0.76)	(1.05)
ReturnSkew			-0.02	-0.02	-0.01	-0.01	-0.01	-0.01
			(-3.92)***	(-2.97)***	(-2.16)**	(-2.44)**	(-1.72)*	(-1.36)
Completed				0.06	0.07	0.05	0.04	0.05
				(3.67)***	(4.60)***	(2.64)***	(2.34)**	(3.05)***
Hostile				0.09	0.09	0.09	0.08	0.09
				(2.67)**	(2.22)**	(2.18)**	(1.98)**	(2.29)**
Tender				0.06	0.05	0.07	0.07	0.06
				(3.81)***	(3.02)***	(3.35)***	(3.47)***	(3.32)***
Rumor				-0.07	-0.09	-0.05	-0.05	-0.06
				(-4.77)***	(-5.70)***	(-3.36)***	(-2.94)***	(-3.45)***
Cash50				0.09	0.08	0.08	0.08	0.07
				(7.45)***	(5.48)***	(5.49)***	(5.36)***	(4.34)***
AcqIndustry				0.01	0.02	0.00	0.00	0.00
				(1.3)	(1.68)*	(0.22)	(0.2)	(0.3)
Size						0.00	0.00	0.00
						(-0.41)	(0.63)	(0.34)
BM						-0.02	-0.02	-0.02
						(-1.90)*	(-2.11)**	(-2.50)**
AcqType						0.05	0.06	0.05
						(3.13)***	(3.37)***	(3.17)***
OptBidAsk							0.12	0.08
							(2.31)**	(1.33)
OptOI							-0.00	-0.00
							(-3.14)***	(-3.74)***
AbnSVol							-0.01	-0.01
							(-2.38)**	(-2.28)**
AbnOVol							0.00	0.00
							(1.13)	(1.23)
Industry fixed effects		YES			YES	YES	YES	YES
Year fixed effects		YES			YES			YES
Intercept	0.15	-0.03	0.16	0.07	-0.04	-0.14	-0.19	-0.15
	22.12***	(-0.29)	(15.94)***	(4.24)***	(-0.49)	(-1.45)	(-2.12)**	(-1.60)
N	994	994	994	842	842	718	714	714
R-square	0.0026	0.1278	0.0353	0.2371	0.3448	0.3263	0.3423	0.3712
Adj. R-square	0.0016	0.0545	0.0314	0.2280	0.271099	0.2580	0.2707	0.2849

The control variables in Table 9 are similar to those in Table 8. The stock price run-up is a little more pronounced (a one standard deviation increase in *return* will lead to a decrease in CAR by up to 4%) and both the *hostile* and the *completed* dummy are statistically and economically more significant in all specifications. Furthermore, the pre-month return skewness seems to be negatively related to CAR (while it was insignificant in all but one of the IV spread models), indicating that option IV skew and past stock return skewness are interrelated. Finally, both option liquidity measures significantly predict lower announcement CARs. This calls into doubt my previous conclusion that the observed relationship might be spurious. Future research should examine this relationship more closely.

Lastly, the regression results for the O/S ratio are reported in Table 10. Chan et al. (2012) and Roll et al. (2010) find evidence for a positive relationship between the *t–1* log-transformed O/S ratio and *absolute* CARs. However, my analysis of target firms reveals no such relation. In particular, the one-day lagged O/S ratio seems to have no statistical significance, no matter whether it is log-transformed or not. To reduce the noise in the trading volume data, I instead regress CAR on the average 5-day (non-log-transformed) O/S ratio. Thus, my results are not directly comparable to the existing literature. Table 10 shows that O/S is negatively – not positively – related to CAR and highly significant in almost all specifications. Increasing the O/S by one standard deviation will decrease CAR by between 0.9% (model 6) and 1.8% (model 1). Using absolute CAR as the dependent variable, the relation is still significant at the 5% level, but the effect is smaller (less than 1% decrease, not tabulated). Also, clustering standard errors by time or industry does not affect the statistical significance considerably.

These results strengthen the conclusions drawn from the sorted portfolio approach and represent one of the main findings of this study: While traders seem to trade primarily in the options markets when they have private information about acquiring firms (cf. Chan et al. 2012), they opt for the stock market if their information concerns a target firm. This finding would contradict Cao et al. (2005) who propose that option markets displace stock markets as the primary venue for informed traders around M&A events. Roll et al. (2010) show that O/S is highly correlated with firm size, i.e. smaller firms will have less option trading relative to stock trading. This accords with intuition since options of small firms have a much lower liquidity, which means that they are not only costly to buy but also more difficult to close out quickly. Closing out a large call position right after a takeover announcement might prove particularly costly because, with the takeover premium being priced in, the call will be deep in-the-money and therefore even less liquid. Despite this result, the question remains why the two control variables for option liquidity predict lower CARs when liquidity is up. Even if only a small number of informed traders use options, the relationship should still be positive. In summary, I can reject hypothesis H2 for IV spread, but not for IV skew and O/S: both of these informed option trading proxies seem to predict announcement CARs for target firms.

TABLE 10: CROSS-SECTIONAL REGRESSIONS OF TARGET CAR ON O/S

This table presents cross-sectional regression results of target announcement returns on the O/S ratio and a number of control variables. The CARs are computed for an event window from *t* to *t+1* with an estimation period of *t-205* to *t-6*, using a 4-factor model. The O/S ratio was calculated by dividing the total option volume over the five days preceding the announcement (multiplied by 100) by the total stock trading volume. All control variables are defined as in Table 8. t-statistics (in parentheses) are reported using White's (1980) heteroskedasticity robust standard errors. *, **, *** denote statistical significance at the 10%, 5%, and 1% level, respectively.

	Dependent Variable: $CAR_{i,[0,1]}$						
	(1)	(2)	(3)	(4)	(5)	(6)	(7)
O/S (5d average)	-0.16	-0.13	-0.10	-0.08	-0.12	-0.08	-0.07
	(-3.67)***	(-3.07)***	(-2.53)***	(-1.98)**	(-2.5)***	(-1.82)*	(-1.64)
Return		-0.03	-0.10	-0.11	-0.12	-0.11	-0.12
		(-0.86)	(-3.01)***	(-3.49)***	(-3.23)***	(-3.04)***	(-3.30)***
ReturnSD		-0.28	-0.08	-0.36	-0.19	0.20	0.05
		(-0.99)	(-0.27)	(-0.97)	(-0.50)	(0.49)	(0.11)
ReturnSkew		-0.02	-0.02	-0.01	-0.01	-0.01	-0.01
		(-3.27)***	(-2.68)***	(-2.15)**	(-1.85)*	(-1.34)	(-1.1)
Completed			0.05	0.05	0.04	0.04	0.04
			(3.99)***	(4.23)***	(2.49)**	(2.60)***	(3.06)***
Hostile			0.03	0.03	0.02	0.01	0.02
			(1.55)	(1.17)	(0.69)	(0.45)	(0.8)
Tender			0.09	0.08	0.09	0.09	0.09
			(6.15)***	(4.93)***	(4.62)***	(4.79)***	(4.49)***
Rumor			-0.07	-0.08	-0.06	-0.05	-0.06
			(-4.39)***	(-4.26)***	(-2.82)***	(-2.58)***	(-2.69)***
Cash50			0.10	0.08	0.10	0.09	0.08
			(8.89)***	(6.49)***	(7.32)***	(6.74)***	(5.73)***
AcqIndustry			0.03	0.04	0.01	0.01	0.01
			(3.16)***	(3.88)***	(1.25)	(0.69)	(1.05)
Size					0.00	0.01	0.00
					(-0.15)	(1.29)	(0.79)
BM					-0.01	-0.01	-0.02
					(-1.21)	(-1.31)	(-1.68)*
AcqType					0.06	0.05	0.05
					(3.04)***	(2.69)***	(2.25)**
OptBidAsk						0.11	0.07
						(3.34)***	(1.82)*
OptOI						0.00	0.00
						(-0.84)	(-1.20)
AbnSVol						-0.02	-0.02
						(-3.73)***	(-3.46)***
AbnOVol						0.00	0.00
						(1.29)	(1.36)
Industry fixed effects				YES	YES	YES	YES
Year fixed effects				YES			YES
Intercept	0.18	0.20	0.09	0.03	-0.08	-0.17	-0.12
	(30.99)***	(21.31)***	(5.81)***	(0.69)	(-1.13)	(-2.42)**	(-1.63)
N	2146	2146	1850	1850	1563	1496	1496
R-square	0.0068	0.0189	0.1635	0.2271	0.2242	0.2398	0.2635
Adj. R-square	0.0064	0.0170	0.1590	0.1881	0.1845	0.1968	0.2130

4.2.3 Deal and target characteristics

In this final section, I test hypotheses 3 to 5 that propose that some traders have special information about the deal or the target. If this informational advantage exists, it should have a moderating effect on the relationship between any of the three informed option trading proxies and target announcement CAR. Specifically, I look at the following characteristics: the percentage of cash used in the transaction (hypothesis H3), entrenchment of target management (H4), and target-bidder industry, i.e. if the target is in the same industry as the bidding firm (H5). But there is another factor that might be of interest: firm size. While size does not seem to predict the takeover premium (see previous regression results) it could be an important determinant of the predictive power of informed option trading proxies. After all, we expect larger firms to have higher option liquidity; and higher liquidity should induce more informed traders to exploit the options' implicit leverage. However, interacting IV spread, IV skew, or O/S with size does not yield significant coefficients (not tabulated). This does not imply that the aforementioned economic intuition is wrong. It only means that the variation in firm size within the sample of target firms is too small to have an impact.

With regard to the financing of the deal, I find some evidence that a higher fraction of cash increases the predictability of options for CARs, which would indicate that traders have information about the financing details. Table 11 shows that the *financing* dummy is negative and highly significant. The coefficient is between –10% and –15%, which is in line with Travlos (1987) and Croci et al. (2012) who argue that the announcement return (or premium) should be lower for stock bids as opposed to cash bids due to the tax-advantage of stock and because a cash offer conveys favorable news about the quality of the target. The interaction term, on the other hand, is only slightly significant (t-stat 1.65) in one of the models (4), which tests the relation between IV skew and CAR. The positive coefficient of 0.28 follows economic intuition: In this model, the conditional effect of IV skew captures the predictability for the base group (*financing* dummy is 0), i.e. cash offers. It has a negative coefficient of –0.31 that is significant at the 5% level. Here, a one standard deviation increase in IV skew would result in a 2.8% decrease in CAR. On the other hand, stock-financed deals only have a coefficient of (–0.31 + 0.28 =) –0.03, which is marginal economically. The model therefore predicts that informed traders buy more ATM call options as opposed to OTM puts if they know the deal is cash-financed. Stock-financed deals might be associated with higher uncertainty about both the premium and the value of the target, which is why the coefficient is close to zero (indicates not much informed trading). For IV spread, the sign of the interaction term and the main effect correspond with intuition. However, this is not the case for the O/S ratio. In either case, the insignificance of the interaction coefficients inhibits me from drawing a meaningful conclusion. In summary, I do not find convincing evidence that informed option traders know about the mode of payment before the offer is announced. Hypothesis H3 therefore needs to be rejected.

TABLE 11: INFORMED TRADING WITH DIFFERING MODES OF PAYMENT

This table shows target announcement CARs regressed on IV spread, IV skew and O/S, respectively, as well as on a financing dummy and an interaction term (PROXY x Financing). CAR, IV spread/skew, O/S and all controls are computed in the same manner as in Tables 8 to 10. PROXY represents either IV spread (models 1 and 2), IV skew (3 and 4) or O/S (5 and 6). Financing equals 1 if the transaction was financed with less than 25% cash and 0 if cash amounted to more than 75% of total financing. t-statistics (in parentheses) are reported using White's (1980) heteroskedasticity robust standard errors. *, **, *** denote statistical significance at the 10%, 5%, and 1% level, respectively.

	Dependent Variable: $CAR_{i,[0,1]}$					
	IV Spread		IV Skew		O/S	
	(1)	(2)	(3)	(4)	(5)	(6)
PROXY	-0.00	0.08	-0.34	-0.31	-0.17	-0.14
	(0.03)	(0.76)	(2.98)***	(2.51)**	(2.61)***	(1.88)*
Financing	-0.13	-0.10	-0.15	-0.10	-0.13	-0.11
	(11.60)***	(5.95)***	(9.20)***	(4.24)***	(9.90)***	(5.76)***
PROXY x Financing	**0.01**	**-0.09**	**0.18**	**0.28**	**0.05**	**0.12**
	(0.08)	**(0.74)**	**(1.26)**	**(1.65)***	**(0.57)**	**(1.30)**
Return		-0.14		-0.18		-0.11
		(3.59)***		(4.62)***		(2.90)***
ReturnSD		-0.08		0.37		-0.25
		(0.17)		(1.10)		(0.58)
ReturnSkew		0.00		-0.01		-0.01
		(0.14)		(0.95)		(1.30)
Completed		0.02		0.06		0.04
		(1.35)		(2.82)***		(2.67)***
Hostile		0.03		0.10		0.03
		(0.82)		(2.06)**		(0.97)
Tender		0.08		0.07		0.08
		(4.27)***		(3.04)***		(3.89)***
Rumor		-0.08		-0.06		-0.05
		(4.62)***		(3.17)***		(2.26)**
AcqIndustry		0.02		0.01		0.02
		(1.68)*		(0.84)		(1.60)
Size		-0.00		-0.00		-0.00
		(0.48)		(0.63)		(0.23)
BM		-0.03		-0.02		-0.02
		(2.78)***		(2.37)**		(1.67)*
AcqType		0.07		0.06		0.06
		(4.37)***		(2.92)***		(2.75)***
Industry/year fixed effects	YES	YES	YES	YES	YES	YES
Intercept	0.11	0.10	0.09	-0.05	0.15	0.01
	(1.89)*	(1.11)	(1.18)	(0.50)	(2.95)***	(0.15)
N	1,470	1,052	860	603	1,886	1,342
R-square	0.1799	0.2649	0.2553	0.3821	0.1698	0.2614
Adj. R-square	0.1315	0.2217	0.1809	0.2846	0.1315	0.2064

According to hypothesis H4, the predictive power of pre-announcement informed option trading may depend on the accuracy of traders' information and could be indirectly associated with the degree of managerial entrenchment. If entrenchment does influence predictability, the interaction term between the informed option trading proxy and the entrenchment proxy (shares held by top-management) should be significantly different from zero. If traders' information is based on facts, the sign of the (combined) coefficient should correspond to what we would expect from the unconditional effect, i.e. positive for IV spread and O/S and negative for IV skew. Otherwise, the sign may be reversed.

Table 12 presents the regression results. For IV spread, the interaction term is positive but insignificant. If target management owns more than 10% of the stock (signals entrenchment), the coefficient of IV spread is between (–0.54 + 0.58 =) 0.04 and 0.21, which is statistically not significant (t-stat 0.1 and 0.4).[4] On the other hand, the coefficient is significantly negative (–0.54) if managerial ownership is below 10%. Since the interaction term is insignificant, hypothesis H4 is rejected for IV spread. The same holds for IV skew. One could argue that the option illiquidity of target firms could prevent traders from trading in the options market regardless of how likely the takeover is. The O/S ratio could shed some light on this question. In fact, both the coefficient of O/S (the conditional effect) and the interaction term have significant coefficients in models 5 and 6. Without entrenchment (*ExecutiveShares*=0), a one standard deviation increase in O/S decreases CAR by 0.15 standard deviations (i.e. –3.38%). If managers are entrenched, a standard deviation increase in O/S will lead to a 1.4% increase in CAR (t-stat 0.78). Following the economic narrative behind hypothesis H4, this would imply that traders who know for a fact that a takeover is coming will disregard the lower probability of a takeover that can be associated with managerial entrenchment. Due to the entrenchment, the better-informed traders expect a higher premium and are therefore more likely to also engage in informed option trading (the higher premium compensates them for the expected loss resulting from low option liquidity). Of course, this conclusion is based on very strong assumptions. But the finding could be a good foundation for future research about information asymmetry surrounding takeovers.

[4] The t-statistic for the combined effect, i.e. for the case where *ExecutiveShares*=1, was determined by flipping over the dummy variable and re-running the regression. The conditional coefficient of the *PROXY* variable then equals the combined effect in the original regression.

TABLE 12: INFORMED TRADING WITH ENTRENCHED TARGET MANAGEMENT

This table shows target announcement CARs regressed on IV spread, IV skew and O/S, respectively, as well as on a dummy proxying for entrenchment (executiveShares) and an interaction term (PROXY x executiveShares). CAR, IV spread, IV skew, O/S and all controls are computed in the same manner as in Tables 8 to 10. PROXY represents either IV spread (models 1 and 2), IV skew (3 and 4) or O/S (5 and 6). ExecutiveShares equals 1 if the estimated percentage of outstanding shares held by top managers and directors (according to the Corporate Library database) exceeds 10%, and 0 otherwise. t-statistics (in parentheses) are reported using White's (1980) heteroskedasticity robust standard errors. *, **, *** denote statistical significance at the 10%, 5%, and 1% level, respectively.

	Dependent Variable: $CAR_{i,[0,1]}$					
	IV spread		IV skew		O/S	
	(1)	(2)	(3)	(4)	(5)	(6)
PROXY	-0.54	-0.31	-0.19	-0.14	-0.27	-0.29
	(-2.36)**	(-1.37)	(-1.56)	(-1.18)	(-4.17)***	(-3.20)***
ExecutiveShares	0.03	0.03	0.01	0.02	-0.01	-0.01
	(1.37)	(1.35)	(0.40)	(0.72)	(-0.50)	(-0.48)
PROXY x ExecutiveShares	**0.58**	**0.53**	**0.10**	**0.04**	**0.30**	**0.42**
	(1.46)	**(0.94)**	**(0.37)**	**(0.13)**	**(2.00)****	**(2.34)****
Return	-0.14	-0.09	-0.31	-0.24	-0.03	-0.00
	(-2.06)**	(1.11)	(-4.96)***	(-3.77)***	(-0.34)	(-0.04)
ReturnSD	0.12	0.69	1.39	1.08	-0.37	-0.14
	(0.13)	(0.53)	(1.96)*	(1.30)	(-0.45)	(-0.14)
ReturnSkew	-0.00	-0.00	-0.01	-0.01	-0.01	-0.01
	(-0.49)	(-0.53)	(-1.19)	(-0.79)	(-1.61)	(-0.86)
Completed	0.01	-0.03	0.03	0.01	0.04	0.00
	(0.34)	(1.32)	(1.64)	(0.29)	(2.06)**	(0.15)
Hostile	-0.04	-0.07	0.03	0.04	-0.02	-0.09
	(-0.99)	(-1.48)	(0.52)	(0.70)	(-0.53)	(-1.64)
Tender	0.09	0.12	0.04	0.07	0.08	0.12
	(3.69)***	(3.95)***	(1.72)*	(2.33)**	(3.16)***	(3.45)***
Rumor	-0.12	-0.07	-0.11	-0.07	-0.10	-0.07
	(-5.23)***	(-2.57)**	(-4.85)***	(-2.65)***	(-4.28)***	(-2.29)**
Cash50	0.10	0.10	0.10	0.09	0.09	0.09
	(5.77)***	(4.99)***	(6.11)***	(4.97)***	(5.67)***	(4.97)***
AcqIndustry	0.04	0.03	0.04	0.03	0.05	0.03
	(2.52)**	(1.57)	(2.35)**	(1.56)	(3.14)***	(1.68)*
Size		-0.00		0.00		-0.00
		(-0.33)		(0.13)		(-0.18)
BM		-0.04		-0.01		-0.01
		(-2.22)**		(-0.66)		(-0.65)
AcqType		0.06		0.05		0.03
		(3.14)***		(2.12)**		(0.82)
OptBidAsk		-0.01		-0.03		-0.04
		(-0.13)		(-0.38)		(0.80)
OptOI		-0.00		-0.00		-0.00
		(-0.82)		(-3.67)***		(-0.10)
AbnSVol		-0.03		-0.01		-0.03
		(-2.94)***		(-1.85)*		(-3.07)***
AbnOVol		0.00		0.00		0.00
		(1.13)		(0.37)		(1.75)*
Industry/year fixed effects	YES	YES	YES	YES	YES	YES
Intercept	0.08	-0.07	0.08	-0.03	0.07	0.00
	(1.47)	(-0.53)	(1.48)	(-0.26)	(1.13)	(0.03)
N	592	471	370	295	740	553
R-square	0.3467	0.4304	0.4893	0.5494	0.3061	0.3721
Adj. R-square	0.2503	0.3136	0.3676	0.3978	0.2243	0.2641

In Appendix 6, I report results for another entrenchment measure, the percentage of outside directors on the board. *Board* is 1 if outsiders account for more than 75% of total directors; it can be associated with less entrenchment. The table shows that the interaction term is negative and significant in both O/S models. For the case of independent boards (dummy=1), the combined coefficient of –0.31 in model 6 means that a one standard deviation increase in O/S will decrease CAR by about 3.5%. If the board is controlled by more insiders, then the coefficient is zero. This is in line with the above results.

In Table 13, I report results for the tests on my last hypothesis H5. If special industry know-how gives traders an informational advantage, the interaction term (*PROXY x acqIndustry*) should be significant. Because we expect this informational advantage to improve the predictability of CARs, the coefficients of the three informed option trading proxies should be more pronounced, with the signs corresponding to economic intuition. That is, IV spread and O/S are positively related to CAR and IV skew negatively. The results show that this is the case for all three proxies. If bidder and target industry are the same (*acqIndustry*=1), IV spread has a coefficient of (–0.05 + 0.23 =) 0.18 in model 2, which is significant with 90% confidence (t-stat 1.87). This implies that a standard deviation increase in IV spread increases CAR by 0.12 standard deviations or 2.4%. By contrast, CAR decreases by 0.6% if the dummy equals zero. For IV skew, only one model (5) is slightly significant. But as expected, the negative relation between the IV skew and CAR is more pronounced if the targets and bidders are from the same industry: The two coefficients for IV skew of –0.03 and (–0.03 – 0.23 =) –0.26 imply that the decrease in CAR (as the result of a one standard deviation increase in IV skew) is over 2% larger if the target and bidder industry are the same, compared to the alternative. Regarding O/S, we also see that the interaction term is not significant, but that it has the predicted sign. On the other hand, the main effect (*acqIndustry*=0) is higher in absolute terms than in Table 10, showing that traders are even more likely to trade in the stock market instead of the options market if they do not have industry-specific knowledge. I conclude that informed option trading seems to be partially driven by traders with special industry know-how. These insiders have an informational advantage that they use to trade in the options market. An alternative interpretation of the result could be that news about a prospective takeover attracts more attention if two firms from the same industry merge, because such a merger could change the power structure within the respective industry. Such a case is more likely to attract the media, which would result in more "informed" trading also by common investors outside the industry. In any case, I cannot reject hypothesis H5.

TABLE 13: INFORMED TRADING WITHIN THE SAME INDUSTRY

This table shows target announcement CARs regressed on IV spread, IV skew and O/S, respectively, as well as on an industry dummy and an interaction term (PROXY x acqIndustry). CAR, IV spread, IV skew, O/S and all controls are computed in the same manner as in Tables 8 to 10. PROXY represents either IV spread (models 1 and 2), IV skew (3 and 4) or O/S (5 and 6). AcqIndustry equals 1 if the target and bidding firm share the same 2-digit SIC code, and 0 otherwise. t-statistics (in parentheses) are reported using White's (1980) heteroskedasticity robust standard errors. *, **, *** denote statistical significance at the 10%, 5%, and 1% level, respectively.

	Dependent Variable: $CAR_{i,[0,1]}$					
	IV spread		IV skew		O/S	
	(1)	(2)	(3)	(4)	(5)	(6)
PROXY	-0.04	-0.05	-0.03	-0.05	-0.12	-0.14
	(-1.52)	(-1.72)*	(-0.34)	(-0.46)	(-2.10)**	(-2.02)**
AcqIndustry	0.02	0.01	0.02	0.01	0.03	0.01
	(2.38)**	(1.07)	(1.61)	(0.80)	(2.19)**	(0.37)
PROXY x AcqIndustry	**0.17**	**0.23**	**-0.23**	**-0.20**	**0.07**	**0.10**
	(1.87)*	**(2.25)****	**(-1.71)***	**(-1.37)**	**(0.95)**	**(1.22)**
Return	-0.14	-0.15	-0.19	-0.16	-0.09	-0.12
	(-4.15)***	(-4.08)***	(-5.41)***	(-4.26)***	(-2.99)***	(-3.29)***
ReturnSD	0.15	0.08	0.68	0.31	-0.25	0.05
	(0.36)	(0.18)	(2.40)**	(0.99)	(0.75)	(0.10)
ReturnSkew	-0.00	0.00	-0.01	-0.01	-0.01	-0.01
	(-0.79)	(-0.22)	(-2.36)**	(-1.38)	(-2.31)**	(-1.09)
Completed	0.05	0.03	0.06	0.05	0.06	0.04
	(3.66)***	(1.89)*	(4.09)***	(3.03)***	(4.37)***	(3.06)***
Hostile	0.05	0.03	0.10	0.09	0.04	0.02
	(2.12)**	(1.04)	(2.70)***	(2.28)**	(1.86)*	(0.82)
Tender	0.08	0.08	0.06	0.07	0.09	0.08
	(5.32)***	(4.76)***	(3.45)***	(3.34)***	(5.44)***	(4.46)***
Rumor	-0.11	-0.08	-0.08	-0.06	-0.09	-0.06
	(-7.98)***	(-4.48)***	(-5.56)***	(-3.38)***	(-5.00)***	(-2.66)***
Cash50	0.09	0.08	0.08	0.07	0.09	0.09
	(7.68)***	(5.98)***	(5.86)***	(4.41)***	(7.40)***	(5.77)***
Size		0.00		0.00		0.01
		(0.26)		(0.30)		(0.82)
BM		-0.03		-0.02		-0.02
		(-3.16)***		(-2.53)**		(-1.69)*
AcqType		0.07		0.06		0.05
		(4.59)***		(3.31)***		(2.28)**
OptBidAsk		0.11		0.08		0.07
		(2.32)**		(1.37)		(1.78)*
OptOI		-0.00		-0.00		-0.00
		(-0.98)		(-3.60)***		(-1.20)
AbnSVol		-0.01		-0.01		-0.02
		(-2.72)***		(-2.27)**		(-3.47)***
AbnOVol		0.00		0.00		0.00
		(0.34)		(1.07)		(1.38)
Industry fixed effects		YES		YES		YES
Year fixed effects	YES	YES	YES	YES	YES	YES
Intercept	0.08	-0.21	0.06	-0.16	0.09	-0.12
	(3.27)***	(-2.53)**	(2.06)**	(-1.72)*	(4.22)***	(-1.61)
N	1447	1230	842	714	1850	1496
R-square	0.2050	0.2930	0.2668	0.3734	0.1828	0.2641
Adj. R-square	0.1898	0.2331	0.2425	0.2863	0.1707	0.2131

In summary, the findings suggest that informed trading might indeed be driven by traders with very specific knowledge about the takeover. This could be an indication of illegal insider trading. However, the results are not very strong statistically and it is not the principal concern of this study to determine whether or not any kind of informed trading should be marked as illegal. The bottom line is that certain deal characteristics can affect the degree of informed trading. It is up to future research to test this result in different settings, for example in the context of earnings announcements.

4.2.4 Significance of the results

With few exceptions, the above findings are in line with economic intuition (i.e. the coefficients of the interaction terms have the expected sign), but are only statistically significant in some cases. It is particularly important to note that even though IV spread, IV skew, and O/S all supposedly proxy for informed option trading, the interaction terms in Tables 11 to 13 are not jointly significant or insignificant. In other words, the findings are not robust across the different proxies used for informed trading. For example, in Table 11 the mode of payment only moderates the relationship between IV skew and CAR, while it has no such effect on the relationship between the other two proxies and CAR. Similarly, only the *O/S-entrenchment* interaction terms have significant coefficients in Table 12. In Table 13, the interaction terms are (slightly) significant in the case of IV spread and IV skew, but not for the O/S proxy. As a consequence, it is difficult to draw a universal conclusion about what information is available to traders, i.e. which hypotheses to reject. In this last section, I want to briefly discuss this issue.

There may be several explanations for the weak statistical results and the inconsistencies across the three proxies. First of all, IV spread and IV skew do not seem to be able to predict target announcement CARs very well, as compared to CARs of bidding firms (see Tables 8 and 9). As discussed before, this may be due to the limited number of target firms with traded options and to the lower option liquidity. Also, small firms are usually not covered by analysts and do not attract much media attention, resulting in less informed trading. Given the low predictive power of these two proxies, it stands to reason that introducing an interaction term will not considerably change the statistical significance of this relation. The fact that IV spread becomes a significant predictor of CARs if the target and the bidding firm are in the same industry (with 90% confidence) emphasizes the strong impact industry affiliation can have on informed option trading. The insignificance of the *O/S-AcqIndustry* interaction term in this framework does not mitigate the implications of this noteworthy result because O/S only captures which markets informed traders trade in, not the direction of the trades. The choice between these two markets can, however, be unrelated to the private information these traders have, e.g. it may be a function of (relative) transaction costs. With regard to industry know-how, I therefore believe that my results are statistically sound and that hypothesis H5 should not be rejected.

In comparison, the moderating effect of the mode of payment (Table 11) is much weaker statistically. Only one out of six interaction coefficients is (barely) significant, which might as well be a statistical fluke. I offer three possible explanations for this result. First, traders may simply have no information about the deal financing. This interpretation would imply that informed trading cannot be equated with insider trading. Second, traders may know about the terms of financing but do not consider this information relevant, e.g. because the uncertainty surrounding a stock-financed offer is negligible as the expected takeover premium is positive in all cases. This alternative hypothesis could be tested more easily using a sample of bidding firms instead of targets. Lastly, the problem could be related to the already mentioned issues researchers face with regard to target firms, most notably sample size. Again, using a larger sample of bidding firms could mitigate this issue.

Finally, the low significance of the *executiveShares* interaction terms in Table 12 can largely be attributed to the small sample size. Because the governance data in WRDS' Corporate Library does not cover all sample firms, the already small IV spread/skew samples are further downsized, which directly affects the statistical significance. Gathering this data manually from proxy statements might yield more conclusive results.

5. Conclusion

This study revolves around the question what kind of information "informed" traders have before a takeover announcement. Is their information based on facts or speculation? Do they know about the details of the transaction, e.g. whether it is financed primarily with cash or with stock? Or do traders with special industry know-how have an informational advantage? I try to answer these questions empirically by combining findings from the traditional M&A literature with asset pricing theories, particularly on the cross-section of options and stocks. Combining these two strands of the literature is the first contribution of this study. The second contribution is the emphasis on target firms. M&A-related corporate finance generally focuses on acquiring firms because they allow researchers to investigate the wealth effects of takeovers, i.e. whether or not an acquisition creates value (e.g. through synergies). Target firms seem to be less interesting subjects in this regard. Their announcement returns are usually highly positive and much less uncertain. It is this feature that should make target firms more attractive to informed traders than bidding firms. The literature finds that the size of the takeover premium may depend on whether cash or stock is offered to target shareholders as well as on the fraction of managerial/institutional ownership (cf. Travlos 1987, Croci et al. 2012, and Bargeron et al. 2008). My third and foremost contribution to the literature is to test if these (and other) target and deal characteristics have an impact on informed trading. Put differently, I try to identify what information informed traders have about these characteristics prior to the takeover announcement.

I use options to examine informed trading because options are forward-looking and empirical evidence suggests that some of the price discovery of stocks takes place in the options market. That is, many papers show that options lead stock prices (e.g. Easley et al. 1998). Following Cremers and Weinbaum (2010), Xing et al. (2010), and Roll et al. (2010), I define three "informed option trading" proxies: IV spread, which is the difference between the implied volatilities of call and put options with the same strike price and maturity; IV skew, which is the difference between the implied volatilities of OTM puts and ATM calls; and the relative option-to-stock trading volume O/S. These proxies are found to predict future stock returns, especially around corporate events such as quarterly earnings announcements and takeovers.

Combining M&A data from SDC Platinum, options data from OptionMetrics, and stock trading data from CRSP, my final sample consists of 2,390 takeover announcements for which the target firm has sufficient past stock and option information available. This sample is matched with accounting data from Compustat, earnings information from I/B/E/S, and corporate governance data from WRDS' Corporate Library.

Because the literature stresses the importance of option liquidity for the predictability of announcement returns (e.g. Chakravarty et al. 2004), the first part of my analysis tests (abnormal) liquidity of target firm options prior to the takeover using open interest and bid-ask spread as proxies. For target firms, liquidity might be a key issue as these firms are often small and their options are only thinly traded. To my knowledge, this has not yet been done in the literature. Using a 50-day benchmark period to compute liquidity on non-event days, I find that abnormal open interest of target firm options is significantly different from zero on the two days before the announcement. Abnormal bid-ask spreads are negative and highly significant on all five days preceding the takeover offer. Relative to their mean benchmark values, open interest increases by up to 11% and bid-ask spreads drop by almost 6%. In a different setting, I use pooled and fixed effects logit models to test whether open interest and bid-ask spread can predict the occurrence of a takeover, i.e. whether they affect the probability that there will be an announcement within the next three days. Open interest is a significant predictor in both models but the economic effect is marginal. The odds of a takeover bid decrease by 12-39% if the bid-ask spread increases by 1. However, this effect is only significant in one of the pooled models and in the FE model if firm size is not controlled for. In fact, size seems to be the most important determinant of takeover probability. Both the abnormal liquidity and logit analysis represent preliminary evidence for the presence of informed option traders prior to a takeover announcement.

A standard event study with four-factor-adjusted abnormal (Carhart) returns, a 200-day benchmark period, and a *t* to *t+1* event window (with *t* being the announcement day) is the centerpiece of my methodology. Following Chan et al. (2012), I regress the two-day cumulative abnormal returns (CARs) separately on *t–1* IV spread and IV skew as well as on the lagged five-day average O/S ratio. I include controls for deal and target firm characteristics and liquidity. Since the three informed option trading proxies vary greatly over time, I also include year-fixed effects. In addition to the regression, I analyze quintile portfolio returns sorted on the three proxies. The results show that IV spread is not a significant predictor of target CARs. The positive relationship that Chan et al. (2012) find for acquirers (as well as for targets using quintile portfolios) cannot be validated by my results. IV spread only has a positive (but still insignificant) coefficient of up to 8% if I use its lagged three-day average. With regard to IV skew, my results are in line with Xing et al. (2010) and Chan et al. (2012). The proxy is negatively related to CAR and significant if I control for year-fixed effects. A one standard deviation increase in IV skew leads to a decrease in predicted CAR by up to 1.4%. The third proxy, O/S, is negatively related to CAR with a confidence level of higher than 95% in all but two models. This finding contradicts Roll et al. (2010) and Chan et al. (2012) who show that O/S is a positive predictor of future returns in general and absolute acquirer CARs in particular. I conclude that that O/S is a good proxy for announcement returns, but that it proxies for informed stock trading rather than informed option trading in the context of target firms. This interpretation supports the notion that target options might simply be not liquid enough to be considered profitable by informed traders. They opt for the stock market instead and pass up the chance to lever their investments. This would also explain why IV spread and IV skew are not as significant as suggested by the previous literature.

Finally, I add interaction terms (moderator dummies) to the regressions to test the impact of deal financing, managerial entrenchment, and industry on the predictive power of each of the three informed trading proxies. The results support theories by Travlos (1987) and Croci et al. (2012) that cash-financed deals have higher premiums than stock-financed ones. The financing interaction terms are insignificant in all but one model. However, they show that IV spread and IV skew are stronger predictors of CARs if cash is used to finance the deal. This corresponds to economic intuition since informed traders that know about the mode of payment are less likely to trade in options if stock is used to finance the deal, which implies more uncertainty and lower premiums. Because of the insignificance of the results, I still must reject the hypothesis that traders are informed about the mode of payment. Based on Stulz (1988), I further argue that higher managerial ownership (i.e. entrenchment) decreases the chances of a successful takeover but increases the premium paid to target shareholders if an offer is made. Accordingly, traders who know for a fact that the offer will occur (e.g. insiders) should trade in options if management is entrenched, while speculators should not. My results back this theory at least for O/S (the interaction terms for IV spread and IV skew remain insignificant). While O/S is negatively related to CAR in the case of no entrenchment, the relation is positive if managerial ownership exceeds 10%. This indicates that better-informed traders engage in option trading because they expect a higher premium (which compensates for the losses resulting from option illiquidity), while less informed traders buy stocks. The results are robust to using the fraction of outside board directors as a proxy for entrenchment. Finally, I show that the predictability of CAR by all three option trading proxies is stronger if the bidder and the target firm are from the same industry. This is significant for IV spread and IV skew and indicates that traders with special industry know-how may have an informational advantage. The overall results show that informed traders seem to have very specific knowledge about future deals and that they make rational trading decisions based on what deal and firm characteristics they encounter.

This study has one key limitation, namely the low liquidity of target options. Target firms are typically smaller than the average bidding firm, they are often not publicly listed, and if they have traded options, those tend to be very illiquid. Most research on informed trading shows that liquidity is a vital factor in the price discovery process. My results confirm this notion. From a sample of 2,390 takeovers only 42% had enough option liquidity to construct the IV skew measure. Also, all informed option trading proxies perform worse than in a setting where liquidity is higher on average (e.g. for acquirers). Other limitations are related to the data. The sample only includes U.S. firms and might therefore be geographically biased. Furthermore, only very little data is available on managerial ownership and corporate governance. Lastly, the explanatory power of both the liquidity (logit) models and the main regressions is limited, indicating omitted variables. These variables, however, are difficult to determine. In summary, the results derived in this study need to be treated with caution, but may prove useful for future research in the field. This research could apply my methodology to a broader sample of corporate events, such as earnings announcements. Interacting firm characteristics with informed trading proxies also does not need to be restricted to the options market. Stock markets are more liquid and contribute a larger fraction to the price discovery process. Abnormal pre-announcement stock trading volume might be a simple but effective proxy for informed stock trading, which my results could be tested on. Finally, future research can estimate at what point, with regard to firm size and liquidity, informed traders decide to move from the options to the stock market, or vice versa.

References

Amihud, Y. (2002), "Illiquidity and Stock Returns: Cross-Section and Time Series Effects," *Journal of Financial Markets,* 5, 31-56.

Amin, K. I.; Coval, J.; Seyhun, H. N. (2004), "Index Option Prices And Stock Market Momentum," *Journal of Business*, 77, 835-873.

Amin, K. I.; Lee, C. M. C. (1997), "Option trading, price discovery, and earnings news dissemination," Contemporary Accounting Research, 14(2), 153-192.

Andrade, G.; Mitchell, M.; Stafford, E. (2001), "New evidence and perspectives on mergers," *Journal of Economic Perspectives,* 15, 103-120.

Asquith, P.; Bruner, R. F.; Mullins, D. W. Jr. (1983), "The gains to bidding firms from merger," *Journal of Financial Economics,* 11, 121-39.

Bali, T. G.; Hovakimian, A. (2009), "Volatility Spreads and Expected Stock Returns," *Management Science*, 55(11), 1797-1812.

Bakshi, G.; Cao, C.; Chen, Z. (1997), "Empirical performance of alternative option pricing models," *Journal of Finance,* 52, 2003–2049.

Bargeron, L. L.; Schlingemann, F. P.; Stulz R. M.; Zutter C. J. (2008), "Why do private acquirers pay so little compared to public acquirers," *Journal of Financial Economics,* 89, 375–390.

Battalio, R.; Schultz, P. (2006), "Options and the Bubble." *Journal of Finance*, 61, 2071-2102.

Bayazitova, D.; Kahl, M.; Valkanov, R. I. (2011), "Value Creation Estimates Beyond Announcement Returns: Mega-Mergers versus Other Mergers," *Working Paper*, available at SSRN 1502385.

Berger, P.G.; Ofek, E.; Yermack, D.L. (1997), "Managerial Entrenchment and Capital Structure Decisions," *Journal of Finance*, 52 (4), 1411-1438.

Betton, S.; Eckbo, B. E.; Thorburn, K. (2008), "Markup pricing revisited," *Tuck School of Business Working Paper*, 2008-45.

Bhagat, S.; Dong, M.; Hirshleifer, D.; Noah, R. (2005), "Do tender offers create value? New methods and evidence," *Journal of Financial Economics,* 76, 3-60.

Black, F. (1975), "Fact and Fantasy in the Use of Options," *Financial Analysts Journal*, 31, 36–72.

Black, F.; Scholes, M. (1973), "The Pricing of Options and Corporate Liabilities," *Journal of Political Economy*, 81(3), 637-654.

Bollerslev, T.; Tauchen, G.; Zhou, H. (2009), "Expected stock returns and variance risk premia," *Review of Financial Studies,* 22(11), 4463-4492.

Bradley, M.; Desai, A.; Kim, E.H. (1988), "Synergistic gains from corporate acquisitions and their division between stockholders of target and acquiring firms," *Journal of Financial Economics*, 21, 3–40.

Brown, S.J.; Warner, J.B. (1985), "Using daily stock returns: the case of event studies," *Journal of Financial Economics,* 14, 3–32.

Carhart, M. (1997), "On the persistence of mutual fund performance," *Journal of Finance*, 52, 57–82.

Cao, C.; Chen, Z.; Griffin, J. (2005), "Informational Content of Option Volume Prior to Takeovers," *Journal of Business,* 78, 1073-1109.

Chakravarty, S.; Gulen, H.; Mayhew S. (2004), "Informed trading in stock and options markets," *Journal of Finance*, 59(3), 1235-1258.

Chan, K.; Chung, Y. P.; Fong, W.-M. (2002), "The Informational Role of Stock and Option Volume," *Review of Financial Studies*, 15, 1049–1075.

Chan, K.; Ge, L.; Lin, T. C. (2012), "Informational content of option trading on acquirer announcement return," *Working paper*, available at SSRN 2022121.

Chesney, M.; Crameri, R.; Mancini, L. (2012), "Detecting Informed Trading Activities in the Options Markets," *Working Paper, Swiss Finance Institute Research Paper No. 11-42,* available at SSRN 1522157.

Cremers, M.; Weinbaum, D. (2010), "Deviations from Put-Call Parity and Stock Return Predictability," *Journal of Financial and Quantitative Analysis*, 45(2), 335-367.

Croci, E.; Petmezas, D.; Travlos, N. (2012), "Asymmetric information and target firm returns," *The European Journal of Finance*, 18(7), 639-661.

Donders, M.; Kouwenberg, R.; Vorst, T. (2000), "Options and earnings announcements: an empirical study of volatility, trading volume, open interest and liquidity," *European Financial Management,* 6, 149-171.

Doran, J. S.; Peterson, D. R.; Tarrant, B. C. (2007), "Is there information in the volatility skew?," *The Journal of Futures Markets*, 27(10), 921-959.

Driessen, J.; Lin, T.; Lu, X. (2012), "Why Do Option Prices Predict Stock Returns?," *Working paper,* available at SSRN 2023336.

Easley, D.; O'Hara, M.; Srinivas, P. S. (1998), "Option volume and stock prices: evidence on where informed traders trade," *Journal of Finance*, 53(2), 431-465.

Eckbo, B.E. (2009), "Bidding strategies and takeover premium: a review," *Journal of Corporate Finance,* 15(1), 149-78.

Fama, E. F.; French, K. R. (1993), "Common Risk Factors in the Returns on Stocks and Bonds, *" Journal of Financial Economics*, 33, 3-56.

Fuller, K.; Netter, J.; Stegemoller, M. (2002), "What do returns to acquiring firms tell us? Evidence from firms that make many acquisitions," *Journal of Finance,* 57, 1763-1793.

Golubov, A.; Petmezas, D.; Travlos, N. (2012), "Financing Irrelevance in Corporate Investment Decisions: Evidence from Acquisitions," *Working Paper*, available at SSRN 1855731.

Hansen, R. G. (1987), "A theory for the choice of exchange medium in mergers and acquisitions," *Journal of Business,* 60, 75-95.

Harvey, C.; Siddique, A. (2000), "Conditional Skewness in Asset Pricing Tests," *Journal of Finance*, 55, 1263-1295.

Hull, J. C. (2012), "Options, Futures, And Other Derivatives," 8th Global Edition, Pearson Education, London.

Jarrell, G. A.; Poulsen, A. B. (1989), "The Returns to Acquiring Firms in Tender Offers: Evidence from Three Decades," *Financial Management*, 18(3), 12-19.

Jayaraman, N.; Mandelker, G.; Shastri, K. (1991), "Market anticipation of merger activities: An empirical test," *Managerial and Decision Economics*, 12, 439-448.

Martinez, V. H.; Rosu, I.; Bester, A. C. (2009), "Option Pricing on Cash Mergers," W*orking paper*, available at SSRN 1364491.

Masulis, R. W.; Swan, P. L.; Tobiansky, B. (2010), "Do Wealth Creating Mergers and Acquisitions Really Hurt Acquirer Shareholders?," *Working Paper*, available at SSRN 1787605.

Merton, R. C. (1973), "Theory of Rational Option Pricing," *The Bell Journal of Economics and Management Science,* 4(1), 141-183.

Mikkelson, W. H.; Partch, M.M. (1986), "Valuation effects of security offerings and the issuance process," *Journal of Financial Economics*, 15, 31-60.

Mitchell, M. L.; Mulherin, J.H. (1996), "The impact of industry shocks on takeover and restructuring activity," *Journal of Financial Economics*, 41, 193-229.

Moeller, S. B.; Schlingemann, F. P.; Stulz, R. M. (2004), "Firm size and the gains from acquisitions," *Journal of Financial Economics*, 73, 201-228.

Moeller, S. B.; Schlingemann, F. P.; Stulz, R. M. (2005), "Wealth Destruction on a Massive Scale: A Study of Acquiring Firm Returns in the Merger Wave of the Late 1990s," *Journal of Finance*, 60(2), 757-782.

Morck, R.; Shleifer, A.; Vishny, R.W. (1990), "Do Managerial Objectives Drive Bad Acquisitions?," *Journal of Finance*, 45(1), 31-48.

Myers, S.; Majluf, N. (1984), "Corporate financing and investment decisions when firms have information that investors do not have," *Journal of Financial Economics,* 13, 187-221.

Newey, W. K.; West, K. D. (1987), "A Simple, Positive Semi-definite, Heteroskedasticity and Autocorrelation Consistent Covariance Matrix," *Econometrica*, 55(3), 703-708.

Ni, S. X.; Pan, J.; Poteshman, A. M. (2008), "Volatility Information Trading in the Option," *Journal of Finance*, 63(3), 1059-1091.

Pan, J.; Poteshman, A. M. (2006), "The Information in Option Volume for Future Stock Prices," *Review of Financial Studies,* 19, 871-908.

Risik, E. A. (2009), "Signaling and Value Creation in Mergers," *Working Paper*, available at SSRN 1712183.

Roll, R. (1986), "The hubris hypothesis of corporate takeovers," *Journal of Business*, 59, 197-216.

Roll, R.; Schwartz, E.; Subrahmanyam, A. (2010), "O/S: The relative trading activity in options and stocks," *Journal of Financial Economics*, 96, 1-17.

Savor, P. G.; Lu, Q. (2009), "Do stock mergers create value for acquirers?," *Journal of Finance,* 64, 1061-1097.

Stephan, J. A.; Whaley, R. E. (1990), "Intraday Price Change and Trading Volume Relations in the Stock and Stock Option Markets," *The Journal of Finance*, 45(1), 191-220.

Stulz, R. (1988), "Managerial control of voting rights: Financing policies and the market for corporate control," *Journal of Financial Economics*, 20, 25-54.

Todorov, V. (2010), "Variance risk-premium dynamics: The role of jumps," *Review of Financial Studies*, 23(1), 345-383.

Travlos, G.N. (1987), "Corporate takeover bids, method of payment, and bidding firm's stock returns," *Journal of Finance,* 42(4), 943-963.

Varaiya N.; Ferris, K. (1987), "Overpaying in Corporate Takeover: The Winner's Curse," *Financial Analysts Journal,* 43, 64-70.

Vijh, A. M. (1990), "Liquidity of the CBOE Equity Options," *Journal of Finance*, 45(4), 1157-1179.

Wang, L. (2009), "Implied Volatilities in Mergers and Acquisitions," *Wharton Research Scholars Journal*, available at http://repository.upenn.edu/wharton_research_scholars/64/, accessed on 25/04/2013.

Xing, Y.; Zhang, X.; Zhao, R. (2010), "What Does the Individual Option Volatility Smirk Tell Us about Future Equity Returns?" *Journal of Financial and Quantitative Analysis*, 45(3), 641-662.

Yan, S. (2011), "Jump risk, stock returns, and slope of implied volatility smile," *Journal of Financial Economics*, 99(1), 216–233.

APPENDIX

APPENDIX 1: SUMMARY STATISTICS FOR ALTERNATIVE CARS AND OFFER PREMIUMS

This table presents summary statistics for alternative CARs and takeover premiums. In Panel A, CARs are computed for an event window from t–1 to t+1. Panel B shows the open-to-close CARs for days t to t+1. For this measure, the daily returns were calculated using the stock's opening price instead of the previous day's closing price. Panel C summarizes the offer price to stock price ratio (minus 1) as reported by SDC. The stock price is the target's price one week prior to the announcement. The ratio represents the offer premium. N is the number of announcements per year, MEAN is the average CAR or offer premium, and SD is the standard deviation of returns.

YEAR	N	MEAN	SD	t-stat	N	MEAN	SD	t-stat	N	MEAN	SD	t-stat
1996	120	14.77%	16.44%	5.40	120	0.15%	9.60%	0.07	91	32.32%	27.06%	11.39
1997	146	15.03%	18.01%	6.36	146	0.63%	8.65%	0.33	132	33.31%	31.43%	12.18
1998	227	14.77%	19.42%	7.39	227	-0.12%	9.70%	-0.07	187	34.19%	35.37%	13.22
1999	247	17.99%	21.07%	8.24	247	0.69%	8.69%	0.38	228	38.06%	33.40%	17.21
2000	212	17.95%	26.73%	7.35	212	-0.44%	10.20%	-0.22	190	38.53%	31.89%	16.66
2001	119	22.05%	32.59%	5.94	119	-0.56%	10.25%	-0.19	104	36.85%	46.89%	8.01
2002	62	15.38%	25.39%	3.30	62	-0.21%	11.60%	-0.06	49	28.55%	40.64%	4.92
2003	73	22.04%	34.55%	6.09	73	0.19%	8.32%	0.07	66	33.75%	33.84%	8.10
2004	89	13.69%	15.59%	4.78	89	-0.18%	4.05%	-0.08	78	26.21%	25.21%	9.18
2005	118	15.27%	19.86%	6.54	118	0.47%	5.16%	0.24	107	25.72%	18.16%	14.65
2006	160	15.85%	14.51%	8.15	160	0.63%	6.43%	0.40	134	26.54%	19.85%	15.47
2007	193	18.45%	20.88%	10.38	193	0.92%	9.24%	0.63	165	25.33%	20.97%	15.52
2008	124	24.26%	41.32%	8.58	124	1.85%	16.87%	0.80	99	28.32%	43.11%	6.54
2009	107	21.83%	34.64%	5.84	107	1.26%	10.47%	0.41	73	45.70%	45.24%	8.63
2010	118	22.70%	21.35%	9.26	118	1.58%	9.29%	0.79	88	39.63%	26.24%	14.17
2011	146	22.34%	24.35%	10.71	146	-0.14%	8.70%	-0.08	114	38.48%	39.45%	10.42
2012	129	23.33%	23.34%	9.41	129	1.23%	7.33%	0.61	92	37.74%	32.48%	11.15
All	**2,390**	**18.48%**	**24.49%**	**29.40**	**2,390**	**0.46%**	**9.43%**	**0.93**	**1,997**	**33.65%**	**33.08%**	**45.46**

APPENDIX 2: CORRELATION OF INFORMED OPTION TRADING PROXIES

This table shows the correlation matrix for IV spread, IV skew, and O/S as defined in Tables 2 to 4.

	IV spread	IV skew	O/S
IV spread	1		
IV skew	–0.3050	1	
O/S	–0.0127	0.0082	1

APPENDIX 3: ABNORMAL OPTION LIQUIDITY, EXCL. EARNINGS WINDOWS

This table shows the abnormal open interest (Panel A) and bid-ask spread (Panel B) for the five days before the takeover announcement. In contrast to Table 5, all days within an 11-day earnings announcement window were excluded from the benchmark period. All other definitions are the same as in Table 5.

Panel A: Abnormal Open Interest

Day	t-5	t-4	t-3	t-2	t-1	t
Abn. Open Interest	514.30	633.88	751.69	811.02	940.99	806.85
SD (in 1,000)	20.30	19.86	20.20	20.93	22.52	21.37
t-stat	1.1202	1.4115	(1.65)*	(1.71)*	(1.85)*	(1.67)*

Panel B: Abnormal Bid-Ask-Spread

Day	t-5	t-4	t-3	t-2	t-1	t
Abn. Bid-Ask Spread	-0.007	-0.008	-0.010	-0.011	-0.016	-0.057
SD	0.155	0.153	0.158	0.162	0.167	0.196
t-stat	(-1.91)*	(-2.41)**	(-2.72)***	(-2.96)***	(-4.36)***	(-12.89)***

APPENDIX 4: QUINTILE PORTFOLIO SORTING (TARGET EQUITY VALUE >500M)

This table shows the average target CARs of quintile portfolios formed on IV spread, IV skew and O/S, respectively, limiting the sample to firms with a market capitalization of more than 500 million (according to SDC data). Variable are defined as in Table 7. t-statistics are in parentheses. *, **, *** denote statistical significance at the 10%, 5%, and 1% level, respectively.

Panel A: IV Spread (t-1)

	Low	2	3	4	High	High-Low
Mean CAR	14.30%	15.71%	15.54%	15.94%	16.03%	1.73%
SD CAR	20.97%	16.97%	14.44%	18.13%	22.51%	-
t-stat	(11.08)***	(15.04)***	(17.49)***	(14.29)***	(11.55)***	(0.91)

Panel B: IV Skew (t-1)

	Low	2	3	4	High	High-Low
Mean CAR	15.24%	14.86%	16.49%	14.90%	12.33%	-2.91%
SD CAR	17.66%	18.06%	17.01%	16.73%	15.40%	-
t-stat	(11.52)***	(10.95)***	(12.93)***	(11.85)***	(10.65)***	(-1.66)*

Panel C: O/S ratio (average t-5 to t-1)

	Low	2	3	4	High	High-Low
Mean CAR	16.33%	18.15%	18.52%	13.73%	12.01%	-4.32%
SD CAR	14.94%	21.32%	19.84%	18.07%	17.36%	-
t-stat	(19.02)***	(14.79)***	(16.25)***	(13.20)***	(12.03)***	(-3.28)***

APPENDIX 5: CROSS-SECTIONAL REGRESSIONS OF TARGET CAR ON 3-DAY AVERAGE IV SPREAD

This table presents cross-sectional regression results of target announcement returns on the three-day average IV spread. The CARs are computed for an event window from *t* to *t+1* with an estimation period of *t-205* to *t-6*, using a 4-factor model. IV spread is the equal-weighted average IV spread from day *t-3* to *t-1*. Daily IV spreads are calculated according to Cremers and Weinbaum (2010). All control variables are defined as in Table 8. t-statistics (in parentheses) are reported using White's (1980) heteroskedasticity robust standard errors. *, **, *** denote statistical significance at the 10%, 5%, and 1% level, respectively.

	Dependent Variable: $CAR_{i,[0,1]}$						
	(1)	(2)	(3)	(4)	(5)	(6)	(7)
IV spread (3d average)	0.08	0.07	0.04	0.06	0.05	0.06	0.07
	(1.06)	(0.98)	(0.61)	(0.84)	(0.64)	(0.72)	(0.87)
Return		-0.05	-0.13	-0.15	-0.13	-0.13	-0.14
		(1.71)*	(4.08)***	(4.49)***	(3.75)***	(3.68)***	(3.84)***
ReturnSD		0.03	0.24	-0.06	-0.06	0.13	-0.03
		(0.09)	(0.64)	(0.15)	(0.15)	(0.30)	(0.06)
ReturnSkew		-0.01	-0.01	-0.00	-0.00	-0.00	0.00
		(2.32)**	(1.43)	(0.52)	(0.78)	(0.13)	(0.32)
Completed			0.04	0.05	0.03	0.03	0.03
			(3.61)***	(3.99)***	(1.87)*	(1.88)*	(2.30)**
Hostile			0.05	0.05	0.04	0.03	0.03
			(2.29)**	(1.84)*	(1.34)	(0.91)	(1.14)
Tender			0.09	0.07	0.08	0.08	0.08
			(5.89)***	(4.81)***	(4.54)***	(4.85)***	(4.64)***
Rumor			-0.09	-0.10	-0.08	-0.07	-0.08
			(6.99)***	(7.28)***	(5.05)***	(4.13)***	(4.52)***
Cash50			0.09	0.08	0.09	0.08	0.08
			(8.27)***	(6.42)***	(6.86)***	(6.44)***	(5.94)***
AcqIndustry			0.03	0.03	0.01	0.01	0.01
			(2.62)***	(3.02)***	(0.83)	(0.81)	(1.21)
Size					-0.00	0.00	0.00
					(0.44)	(0.74)	(0.37)
BM					-0.01	-0.01	-0.01
					(1.05)	(1.08)	(1.33)
AcqType					0.07	0.08	0.07
					(4.92)***	(5.22)***	(4.59)***
OptBidAsk						0.11	0.08
						(2.79)***	(1.73)*
OptOI						-0.00	-0.00
						(0.91)	(1.06)
AbnSVol						-0.01	-0.01
						(2.89)***	(2.64)***
AbnOVol						0.00	0.00
						(0.31)	(0.21)
Industry fixed effects				YES	YES	YES	YES
Year fixed effects				YES			YES
Intercept	0.16	0.17	0.08	0.01	-0.10	-0.16	-0.13
	(34.84)***	(18.02)***	(5.01)***	(0.24)	(1.27)	(2.33)**	(1.72)*
N	1758	1758	1518	1518	1294	1283	1283
R-square	0.0008	0.0123	0.1728	0.2458	0.2367	0.2547	0.2845
Adj. R-square	0.0002	0.0100	0.1673	0.1993	0.1897	0.2058	0.2226

APPENDIX 6: INFORMED TRADING WITH ENTRENCHED TARGET MANAGEMENT (2)

This table shows target announcement CARs regressed on IV spread, IV skew and O/S, respectively, as well as on a dummy proxying for entrenchment (board) and an interaction term (PROXY x board). CAR, IV spread, IV skew, O/S and all controls are computed in the same manner as in Tables 8 to 10. PROXY represents either IV spread (models 1 and 2), IV skew (3 and 4) or O/S (5 and 6). Board equals 1 if the fraction of outside/independent directors on the board of directors is higher than 75%, and 0 otherwise. t-statistics (in parentheses) are reported using White's (1980) heteroskedasticity robust standard errors. *, **, *** denote statistical significance at the 10%, 5%, and 1% level, respectively.

	Dependent Variable: $CAR_{i,[0,1]}$					
	IV spread		IV skew		O/S	
	(1)	(2)	(3)	(4)	(5)	(6)
PROXY	-0.10	0.02	-0.09	0.04	0.04	-0.00
	(-0.37)	(0.09)	(-0.72)	(0.29)	(0.34)	(-0.01)
Board	0.00	-0.00	0.01	0.03	0.02	0.03
	(0.12)	(-0.16)	(0.45)	(1.18)	(1.13)	(1.32)
PROXY x Board	**-0.84**	**-0.53**	**-0.16**	**-0.47**	**-0.32**	**-0.31**
	(-1.74)*	**(-0.89)**	**(-0.66)**	**(-1.70)***	**(-2.71)*****	**(-2.34)****
Return	-0.14	-0.11	-0.30	-0.25	-0.00	0.00
	(-2.03)**	(-1.32)	(-4.60)***	(-3.81)***	(-0.02)	(0.01)
ReturnSD	0.31	0.61	1.60	0.82	-0.30	-0.21
	(0.31)	(0.43)	(2.06)**	(0.99)	(-0.35)	(-0.21)
ReturnSkew	-0.00	-0.00	-0.01	-0.01	-0.01	-0.01
	(-0.23)	(-0.42)	(-1.34)	(-0.88)	(-1.57)	(-0.93)
Completed	0.00	-0.04	0.03	0.00	0.03	-0.01
	(0.07)	(-1.61)	(1.31)	(0.14)	(1.70)*	(-0.26)
Hostile	-0.03	-0.06	0.03	0.04	-0.03	-0.10
	(-0.83)	(1.29)	(0.46)	(0.69)	(-0.69)	(-1.78)*
Tender	0.09	0.12	0.04	0.06	0.08	0.12
	(3.71)***	(4.04)***	(1.63)	(2.29)**	(3.31)***	(3.46)***
Rumor	-0.13	-0.08	-0.11	-0.06	-0.10	-0.07
	(-5.46)***	(-2.84)***	(-4.91)***	(-2.58)**	(-4.62)***	(-2.53)**
Cash50	0.10	0.10	0.11	0.09	0.09	0.10
	(5.84)***	(5.15)***	(6.07)***	(4.90)***	(5.75)***	(4.90)***
AcqIndustry	0.04	0.03	0.04	0.04	0.05	0.04
	(2.46)**	(1.48)	(2.21)**	(1.91)*	(3.06)***	(1.84)*
Size		-0.01		-0.00		-0.00
		(-0.52)		(-0.14)		(-0.23)
BM		-0.04		-0.01		-0.01
		(-2.32)**		(-0.64)		(-0.58)
AcqType		0.06		0.04		0.03
		(3.20)***		(1.74)*		(0.80)
OptBidAsk		-0.01		-0.05		-0.04
		(-0.08)		(-0.69)		(-0.77)
OptOI		-0.00		-0.00		-0.00
		(-0.76)		(-3.57)***		(-0.17)
AbnSVol		-0.03		-0.01		-0.03
		(-3.06)***		(-2.02)**		(3.46)***
AbnOVol		0.00		0.00		0.01
		(1.41)		(0.42)		(2.31)**
Industry/year fixed effects	YES	YES	YES	YES	YES	YES
Intercept	0.09	-0.04	0.08	0.01	0.07	0.02
	(1.74)*	(-0.32)	(1.42)	(0.09)	(1.27)	(0.13)
N	589	471	366	293	734	552
R-square	0.3476	0.4304	0.4873	0.5556	0.3055	0.3737
Adj. R-square	0.2507	0.31352	0.3657	0.4075	0.2227	0.2657